AAMIR KHAN
A Social Spark

Dr. Kirti Sisodia

PRABHAT
PRAKASHAN

Published by
PRABHAT PRAKASHAN PVT. LTD.
4/19 Asaf Ali Road,
New Delhi-110 002 (INDIA)
e-mail: prabhatbooks@gmail.com

ISBN 978-93-5266-118-3
AAMIR KHAN : A Social Spark
by Dr. Kirti Sisodia

Edition
2025

Price
₹ 400.00 (Rupees Four Hundred only)

Printed at
Jai Laxmi Printers Press, Delhi

AAMIR KHAN
A Social Spark

Meaning of Aamir:

Aamir is an indirect Quranic name
for boys that means 'prosperous', 'full of life',
'one who has a long and prosperous life'.

"To my parents
for raising me to believe that
everything was possible
To my husband
for making everything possible."

Preface

Passion is the most powerful driving force, when it comes to satisfying once creative urge. This holds true to most of the off-beat heroes in our society, who have got world-wide acclaim. We can easily pin-point such heroes in any fraternity, be it entertainment, literature, sports, technology, trade, business and what not, so to speak.

Talking about Indian silver-screen, there are very few off-beat heroes, who have, more often than not, flabbergasted the audience with their creative genius. If we make a who's who of such heroes, Aamir Khan's name strikes instantly to ones memory. And the reason is quite apparent. He is not just another actor, roaming around the trees, dancing with the co- actresses, or for that matter, getting better off the bunch of villains, and that too absolutely empty-handedly.

Well, these typical sequences have been the most repetitive phenomenon in almost every second Hindi movie over the years. Aamir Khan does not seem to be very fond of doing such routine movies. Of course, for entertainment sake, he also does the dancing, singing and all that. However, most of the Aamir Khan's movies make a deep imprint in the minds of the cine-viewer, even if the message is a subtle one. This definitely underlines the fact, that Aamir Khan relishes to use the art of cinematography for bring about a social change, whatever little it might be.

Right from "Lagaan" to "Taare Zameen Par" to "Three Idiots" and many other movies, Aamir Khan has been terribly choosy in accepting the story-idea of any particular film. Even his Television show "Satya Meva Jayate", was not just a source of making fast bucks either, as many of the other small-screen shows turn out to be. Rather, this instantly popular show became a source of inspiration, to improving many public services like health, education, child abuse, to name a few.

When an actor carries such a distinguished profile and at the same time leaves his fans mesmerized also, thanks to his spontaneous acting and immaculate sense of timing, it automatically and thoroughly deserves to be documented in shape of a social research.

Acknowlegdement

It's my prerogative and extreme pleasure to pace my very first step in the world of writing through this book which has been inspired my Ph. D thesis.

I have always been in love with playing with words to express my feelings but I never thought that I would create this beautiful world of words like this.

I am certain this is my beginning and the start of my unstoppable journey of writing. Although I have been in love with writing, reading but as I believe one needs a catalyst to expedite the reaction.

Various hearts and hands have generously supported the writing and publication of this book. My soulful expression of gratitude starts from my father Mr. V.S. Chouhan, who had ever inspired me for continuous learning and encouraged me always to follow my dreams with passion no matter what conditions, be, to my mother Mrs. K. Chouhan who had shaped my life and always strived hard to compose me into what I am today.

Apart from my parents' support, I strongly

believe I was a raw stone which has been polished and crafted by my husband Vikram Sisodia, who believed in me more than myself and encouraged me to follow my passion.

Not to forget my kids Navni and Shourya for being always so supportive in their own ways. Without their moral support it would not be possible for me to be where I am today.

Last but not the least my brother Anand & bhabhi Megha. Of course my in-laws who have gifted me a golden heart in my life...my husband.

I remain ever grateful to all my friends, colleagues and publishers.

Foreword

"He has a penchant for perfection and professionalism."

"A Method Actor with a penchant for detailing."

"He has taken acting to a whole new level."

"Follows his heart and gives his best to whatever he commits to – movies, social cause, public commitments."

"Man of unconventional but brilliant ways."

"The game changer."

Some of the things that come to mind of people when think of Aamir Khan – the actor, director and social catalyst.

A Padma Shri (2003) and Padma Bhushan (2010) awardee, an honorary doctorate for contribution to Indian cinema, four National Awards for himself, eight National Awards for his movie *Lagaan* that he produced and acted in, numerous Indian film awards, nomination and making into final five in Oscar list of Best Foreign Language film (2002). These are some of the laurels in Aamir Khan's distinguished career.

December 2001, he was declared Man of the year by *Bombay Times*.

In year 2002, he played a Jury's role at Lo Carlo Film Festival.

In year 2004, he, along with Sachin Tendulkar, lead National Voters campaign in Maharashtra.

In March 2007, he was adjudged 3rd most powerful Indian film star by *FORBES*.

In year 2009, NDTV channel and CNN-IBN declared Aamir as the Indian of the year.

In year 2013, he led UN International Children's Emergency Fund in India after Amitabh Bachchan and Priyanka Chopra.

In August 2012, he featured on the cover of *Time* Magazine – Chosen for raising social awareness in India.

A.R. Rehman stated "In a world of false diplomacy and evasiveness, Aamir is a straight forward man. He uses his gifts as a charmer to give his audience the most bitter medicine, hypnotised we take it without complaint. Aamir has started a movement that will help change the world on which Indian live. Jai Ho!" added the Academy winner composer.

It is worth mentioning that in April 2013, he made it to the *Time* magazine list of 100 Most Influential people in the world and he was listed under "Pioneers" Titans/Leaders/Artistes/ Pioneers/Icons.

His TV show *Satyamev Jayate* was part journalism based, part talk show. It confronted India's deepest social ills, from sexual abuse to caste discrimination. He started the movement to have courage to share and ask uncomfortable questions to help change the world Indian live in for a better tomorrow.

Besides being a social catalyst and an actor, Aamir has been a family man, a marketing wizard, an impressionable brand ambassador and much much more that you would find in the book that is my tribute to the Man who brought about social change in the movies and his surroundings.

Introduction

Cinema has the ability to combine entertainment with communication of ideas to the people. It has the potential appeal for its target audience. It certainly leaves other media far behind in making such an impact. As in literature, cinema has produced much which touches the innermost layers of human. It reflects the episodes in such a manner that leaves an impact on the coming generations. Indian Cinema presents an image of the society in which it is born and the hopes, aspirations, frustration and contradictions present in any given social order.

There are variable views about the effects of cinema in our society. Producers and financiers consider it as a tempting and lucrative business. For actors and actresses, it is a means to earn money and popularity among masses. The director, story-writer, song-writer and cinematographer take it as an art work.

Human has instincts, different thoughts flow which leaves an effect on the minds. The person laughs with the films and tears with them. Scenes of Lagaan, a film by Aamir makes people national-minded and sentimentally involved in the film show. The film dialogues are occupying places in our real life.

It is always good and well groomed to see good subjects on cinema. They have a very positive and long-lasting effect on the minds whereas cheap and shabby movies affect the tender minds of audience very badly. When those film makers and actors gain so much fame, glamour and financial aspect, they too must realize having some moral responsibility to return back it to society in good terms. Few film makers and actors do that; one of them is Aamir Khan.

Though he started his career as a commercial actor in Qayamat Se Qayamat Tak with his bushy eyebrows, he produced a lots of movies later like Lagaan, Rang De Basanti, 3 Idiots, Tare Zameen Pe, PK. All these movies reflected the very sensitive issues as prevalent in the present day society.

Cinema is the barometer of the society. Whatever is happening around is duly being portrayed by cinema. All of us would realize that it is a great platform to communicate with masses. And as we Indians follow cinema and various trends that are in vogue are actually shown or set by actors and actresses on Fashion, Hair style, Songs, Music. These things become part of our life and grow of paramount importance as it means cinema not only affects our mind but sometimes also our happiness, sorrows and other emotions also. With cinema as a part of our lives and we tend to live in the scintillating world of cinema thus we emulate. And at this juncture it becomes the duty or social responsibility of our filmmakers that they must put these issues under the scanner and create the right kind of awareness amidst people in the contemporary society.

Talking especially of Aamir films when we talk about Jo Jeeta Vo Sikandar, Lagaan, 3 Idiots, Tare Zameen Pe, Rang De Basanti, PK and of course how can we forget the popular TV Series Satyamev Jayate, Aamir picked up those sensitive issues which remained usually untouched or unexplored before the society in terms of cinema and he dealt with those social issues in his TV program Satyamev Jayate which is already present in our society and our homes long back and still survive. His program on such critical issues gave light of awareness and when youth saw these true stories, victims, conditions and consequences, they came to know directly or indirectly that it is happening in our homes too.

Cinema and TV presents a great platform to stage these kinds of social issues in front of contemporary society and the people. We are living in an electronic era where our new generation who is just a click away from every information. Further very smartly for business transactions we have created so many video games that remain didactic too.

Today one can easily find in the market visual series of Ramayan, Mahabharat, Panchtantra and many more. And in that way at least few will watch otherwise nobody wants to read the Holy Scriptures. Similarly the issues which have been raised by Aamir's cinema and TV shows also draw attention which already existed in society and the spectacular way he has presented those issues in films which not only entertained us but also were showcased beyond being as mundane topics.

During my meeting with him I asked him how to choose the subject of any film; then, he said, " Jo mujhe achchha lagta hai, mere mann ko choo jata hai". I think we all at some or the other point of life come across such situations touched by many things or emotions, but as a common man do not have that audacious platform and of course lack that creative angle to make such interesting, entertaining and informative episodes that our society compels us to watch and commands never to run away from its impact. This kind of thinking doesn't come in a single day or in few days and are never accidental. How Aamir grew his struggles and experiences that he has seen thus far, and how he has evolved into an actor, person and how his films create awareness among the people of society and create an impact too remain all about the scripting of this book.

This book is not about the person; it is about the way of thinking and urge to serve something to society and take those brave steps which can be lethal too for an actor.

Every human has this hidden courage but only a few identify and execute this in a positive way. Human has lots of lacuna but through this book I want to focus only the positive aspect so we can get positive direction.

—Dr. Kirti Sisodia

Contents

Courtesy : Aamir Khan @ Twitter

Courtesy : Google photos

Bande hain hum uske, hum pe kiska zor...
ummeedon ke suraj, nikale chaaron ore...
Iraade hain fauladi, himmati har kadam...
Apane haathon kismat likhne, aaj chale hain hum.

(DHOOM 3)

1

Tete-À-Tete with Aamir: Year 2015

Looking back, I distinctly remember the year, it was 1998. I had appeared for my secondary exams the year Aamir Khan's *Qayamat Se Qayamat Tak* (*QSQT*) released. The girls from my school and neighbourhood would swoon over the chocolate face and innocent looks of the debutant hero but I remained passive to all of it. Being born in a Rajput Family, I had grown up listening to the stories of gallantry and bravery of legendary heroes like Maharana Pratap and Prithviraj Chouhan. The *QSQT* shy boy with bushy eyebrows and large ears did not fit into my quintessential definition of a hero and I remained detached from the euphoria around the new craze called Aamir Chocolate Khan.

Who would have thought that 27 years from that day, I would do my Ph.D. on his work and later pen down a book on his life and works. First impression wasn't really the last impression in this case as I grew liking him as an actor after watching his intense performance as Sanjay Lal Sharma, a good for nothing recluse who transformed into a winner in *Jo Jeeta Wohi Sikander* and some of the other movies that followed. That year was 1992 and since then, I have keenly observed his growth as an actor, an individual and a social mascot.

Before I met him, I was just an admirer of his socially- relevant movies and of the efficiency with which he presented his belief to his devoted audience that found instant connect to his kind of cinema. During my Ph.D., I tried reaching out to him to get his expert views on my research topic "Can films really be a big platform to convey any social message among the people of society " but since he was busy with the promotion of his film *PK* in December 2014 and unavailable to meet at that point of time, I sent my thesis for completion binding. His P.A. during our conversation had assured me that he will meet me post release of the movie.

I took his assurance with a pinch of salt and attributed the excuse for delay of meeting to another starry tantrums of a superstar of the Bollywood but to my utter surprise, his P.A. called up after a month and asked if I would like to come to Mumbai to meet Aamir Khan regarding my thesis.That moment defined Aamir's sincerity to me as a person.

Finally, I met him on 26 February 2015. I was in quandary over what kind of interaction to expect from a man known for his private persona. In this turmoil, I reached 601, Freeda One, 3-a Carter Road at 12:50 pm. His apartment was guarded by black commandos and someone accompanied me to his living room. The room reflected persona of the man – Suave, simple yet elegant, uncluttered like the man himself.

A household help came and asked for tea/ coffee that I politely declined. After 10 minutes wait, the man in simple track pants and T-shirt emerged from a side door and shook my hands. There was an instant connect with Aamir and I felt certain familiarity in his mannerism which was endearing and respectful at the same time.

He was inquisitive about my research topic and said "So Kirti ji, you have came from Raipur, Chhattisgarh and you are doing your Ph.D. That is wonderful. How can I help you?" I was taken back by his gentleness and managed to say few words. He talked to me about his upcoming film *Dangal* and shared how he has been gaining weight for the biopic on the wrestler Mahavir Singh Phogat.

We discussed about my Ph.D., he gave his views on the topic. I was suffering from a cough bout and he called up his staff to bring me warm water. His gesture, however simple, defines the character of a man who is sensitive and considerate to the needs of the others.

The meeting was scheduled for 20 minutes as conveyed by his P.A. but it lasted for over an hour. After discussing the issues related to my Ph.D., society, content of his films and other works, he was keen to discuss the Naxalite problem in Chhattisgarh and also enquired about my family background, family and work. I asked him how he chooses his subjects for the movies and he said he follows his heart to take a decision, however unconventional the subject may seem.

After an hour, I thanked him for his time and had not envisaged him to walk along with me as I left, to accompany me in the elevator and see me off upto the main gate of his apartment building. I was really touched by his kind gesture. At the gate, he politely enquired if I had a vehicle? He stayed on the gate till my car moved. I was pleasantly shocked and surprised with the humility shown by the man of his stature. Aamir Khan, the human being indeed stood tallest in my eyes for his 5′6″ lean frame that day onwards.

My personal interaction with Aamir left an indelible impression on my mind about the man and his sensitive persona. I could comprehend how he can tackle complex human emotions with great sensitivity in his movies and social causes that he endorses. One needs to feel and have a deeper connect with his own emotional being to be able to connect with others in his life and society, a feat mastered by Aamir, the sensitive man who finds an inroad straight into your heart with his humane qualities.

At this onset, I would like to say that this meeting completely transformed my perception about him and his movies. During my Ph.D., I saw his movies with a very different angle and learnt the nuances behind every song and character to understand the understated social message behind them. Various ups and downs in the life through professional and personal challenges have not made him bitter but a better person. He rose like a phoenix when he found his mojo and has continued to rise since then.

What I can say – If you are a good, sensitive and aware person with a gentle heart, it will reflect in your personality and work. After meeting him I could add 'wise' to the list of adjectives that define the legend who featured in the *Time* Magazine's list of "100 Most Influential People in the World" in April 2013.

He is an ace actor, director, producer, television personality, social worker, screenwriter, philanthropist, a husband, a father, a family man. He is a Padma awardee, A national Film Award winner, an Oscar Nominee for his film *Lagaan*. There is much more to the man than his movies and the roles, the accolades and recognition bestowed upon him along with love of millions of fans across the globe as you would discover further in the book.

Happy Reading!

□

praise for the commitment shown by the actor known to be Mr. Perfectionist of Bollywood.

Aamir weighed 68 kgs with 9% body fat for his December 2014 blockbuster hit movie *PK* that turned out to be highest grossing and since then, he has added over 25 kilos of weight during his training for the role of a wrestler in *Dangal*. Such is the passion and commitment of the man for his work that he took the actors who would enact roles of his two wrestler daughters in the movie under his wing. The girls trained and stayed with Aamir and his wife Kiran at their apartment during all these months and Aamir personally supervised the training regime.

The Punjab schedule is for four months and Aamir was spotted entering the airport holding a copy of book *Sapiens: A Brief History of Mankind* by Yuval Noah Harari in his hand and a copy of Avirook Sen's *Aarushi* as he reached his hotel in Punjab. An avid reader, Aamir, by his own admission, prefers reading over watching movies or socialising. A thinking actor who broadened his horizon through the learning he derives from the spectrum of books he reads.

Mahesh Bhatt's son and celebrity fitness trainer, 32-year-old Rahul Bhatt, who has accompanied Aamir for the shooting at Punjab feels inspired to be training the Mr. Perfectionist Khan and taking care of his diet for the role of *Dangal*. Rahul told

Courtesy : Aamir Khan @ Twitter

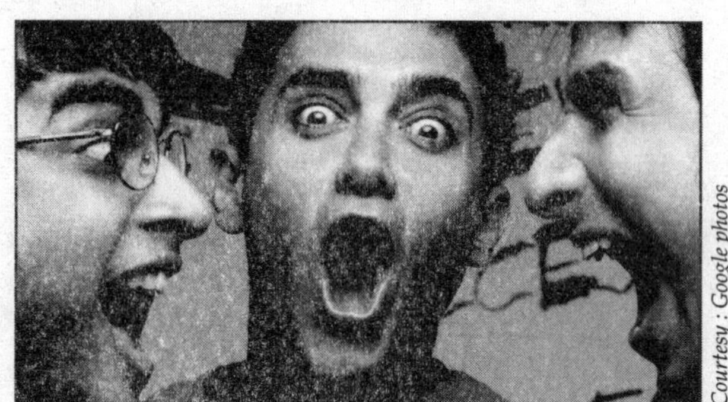

Life is a race ... if you don't run fast ... you will be like a broken andaa.

(3 IDIOTS)

2

Aamir Khan's Childhood and Cinematic Career

"Film-making is like fighting a war with leadership at the front."

—Aamir Kha

September 2015

Villages Kila Raipur and Gujjarwal nea Ludhiana, Punjab have been converted to replicat Villages of Haryana for Aamir Khan's next fil *Dangal*, a biopic on wrestler Mahavir Singh Phoga

Gautam Gulati, the winner of *Big Boss* Seaso 8 chanced upon meeting Aamir Khan on his wa to Amritsar in the flight, posted a selfie with hi on social media and also shared that the legendar actor who weighs 90 kilo plus now faced breathin problems and had difficulty in walking due t the weight.

"Who else can show such dedication for a rol but Aamir Khan." He ended the note with a lavis

Hindustan Times in an interview that Aamir is a dedicated listener and follow the regime to perfection, for exercise and diet both. He does not interfere in his trainings or diet instructions.

In the coming months, Aamir Khan has to regain his normal weight (60-70 kilos) within five months and shall undergo highly-intensive training.

Aamir Khan is a man of conviction. He loves to accept challenges, listens to his heart and has never been scared of unconventional modes of working. Turning 50 earlier this year was another milestone in his life but he shows no signs of slowing down. He is aware of the health hazard sudden weight gain can pose to his health but he is also passionate about the role he has chosen to bring alive on the 72 mm screens in the year 2016.

The mantra that he adopted towards his work and life many years back has guided him with the purpose of his life. He is relentlessly and untiringly walking towards his goal, one step at a time. He feels there is still a long journey ahead of him and he has much more to achieve.

A journey that started in the maternity ward of the Holy Family Hospital in Bandra, Mumbai on 14th March 1965 on the day of festival of colour, Holi.

Flashback: Childhood, Schooling and Film Career Launch

Born to producer Tahir Hussain and his first

wife Zeenat Hussain, Mohammed Aamir Hussain Khan was second of the four children of the couple. The other children were Nikhat Khan, Faisal Khan and Farhat Khan. His childhood was spent in close proximity of his extended family which also had family of his paternal uncle, Nassir Hussain, a director and producer.

Since his father was a producer who during his career produced movies such as *Caravan, Anamika, Zakhmee, Janam Janam Ka Saath, Dulha Bikata Hai, Khoon Ki Pukaar, Locket,* etc, there was a constant inflow of people visiting the house to narrate their stories. Aamir loved storytelling and had a huge appetite to listen to all kinds of stories. He would find a quiet corner in the room where narration would take place and absorb the stories being told.

As a toddler, he was much adored in the neighbourhood and he revealed under the affection he received. He was sent to a girl's school, Ava bhai Petit near his house for Kindergarten and later moved to St. Anne School in Bandra where he studied till VIIth Standard.

Once there was a race and his neighbours had come to cheer him up. The ladies raised their hands to encourage him and he came running towards them thinking they were calling him to take in their affection. It was only after the race was over, he realised he had missed participating in it.

Aamir's mother Zeenat recalls how Aamir

was a self- sufficient streak and insisting on doing everything himself, be it tying his shoelaces or wearing a shirt, even sewing a broken button on it. He detested any help offered, how much struggle it may have been to achieve a task himself. She is very proud of the fact that Aamir was a courteous child who respected everyone, a quality that seeped deep into his psyche and one that he has retained even till date.

Aamir was quality conscious even as a child. His mother once heard him dropping something on the road from their balcony and upon enquiring, she found him clutching on to a fistful of recently released low weight 10 paisa aluminium coins that he was dropping one by one on the road. By the time she heard the tinkering voice, he had finished throwing all of them down the balcony. She asked him "Why were you throwing the coins away?"

"Ye Bekaar Hain" (These are useless) was his answer dusting his hands with the satisfaction of being able to get rid of useless clutter.

A *jumla* (quote) he was often heard saying later in life, for all that did not meet the high standards he had set for his work. Setting the tone for what person he would grow into – a man who is disinterested in all *'bekaar'* things. Once he was established as a famous star, he used this quote to categorise all popular film awards which he thought were unfair and biased (justifiably so) *"Yeh sab bekaar hai"*.

He is a focused man of substance who does not look at life on the surface but believes in dwelling into the depth of things and do extensive work. No fluff worked for him ever since his childhood. He has a no nonsense approach to life and his work, something that has worked for him to be the socially conscious human being that he is known as, even before his stardom comes in the picture.

Growing Up Years

Tahir Hussain went through a financial turmoil as some of the movies he had produced did not perform very well on the silver screen. The money was scarce in the house and there were four school going children to be tended to. Children had witnessed the lenders calls for recovery of money loaned for the movies.

Zeenat Hussain was an able woman who kept her children grounded and did not make them feel deprived under tough circumstances. Even though the house had a car, children travelled by bus or train. Aamir tweeted on micro-blogging site Twitter on Oct. 4, 2014 "My mother is my biggest inspiration."

He also wrote "My mother used to tell me (as a child) "*Ummeed Pe Duniya Chalti Hai*". (Hope makes the world go round).

He used '*#Mumkin Hai*' as the tagline for his TV show *Satyamev Jayate* later and it trended worldwide on twitter on October 4, 2014.

He remains close to his mother to date and she lives in an apartment above his house, to ensure that she is around him, with him and his family.

To help combat family's financial constrain, Aamir, at the age of seven acted as a child artiste in 1973 movie *Yaadon Ki Baraat* that was produced by his uncle, Nassir Hussain.

In the year 1974, he played the younger version of actor Mahendra Sandhu in *Madhosh,* again produced by his uncle, Nasir Hussain.

Aamir was a shy and emotional as a child. He detested all the noise and hullabaloo on the sets. There would be wires all over the sets and people walking all around which depleted the energies of the sensitive child. He did not like the makeup that was put on his face during the shooting. Thus, he refused to act in any movie after *Madhosh* and channelled all his energies to his studies.

He was a bright child and had a sharp brain. He solved Rubik's cube in 28 seconds at the young age of ten. He was a voracious reader. As per Aamir, he would make a top tower of jam sandwiches and lock himself in the rooms with books and magazines he would get from the stores and local libraries. A habit, he has retained till date. He loves to read about history and non-fiction along with fiction. It is rarely a site to see Aamir without a book in hand during his travels. He was a real trickster.

Aamir does not watch many movies but has keen interest in old Hindi movies and is well verse with trivia of movies. He liked Dilip Kumar, Guru Dutt, Waheeda Rehman and Geeta Bali amongst actors of Golden era. He was a big Bimal Roy (da) fan.

AfterClass VIIth,hemovedtoprestigiousScottish High School to study under an ISCE curriculum. He was an avid sportsman and needed a school who had good sports facilities. A keen chess player and also a seeded Maharashtra Sub Junior level player who represented Maharashtra at National games in Tennis during his young days. He played in Tennis circuit and won prizes in many matches. Such was his dedication that he would practice tennis for five hours in a day. The Hindi adage *'Honhaar ke hotey cheekney paat'* (The bright child shines as a toddler) was truly applicable on Aamir.

Director Ashutosh Gowarikar recalls how he observed a young Aamir play Tennis at the Khar Gym where he would go to practice Tennis and realised how good Aamir was at his game. Aamir was already playing under 12 or 14 on state level. One day, Aamir had come early and was practicing on locker rooms while waiting for his partner to come. Ashutosh offered to play with him but Aamir refused stating that it would spoil his game. Ashutosh thought it was a rude comment till he saw Aamir at his game in the court. He realised while he was still a novice, he could see the ease with which Aamir defeated his opponent on the court with finesse of a trained player.

There was another side of Aamir that only people close to him knew of. Behind his emotional and shy persona, there was a real prankster and a charmer hidden who would use his wits and brain to conquer any kind of situation. His cousins and younger siblings were easy targets for his pranks. He would trick his younger brother and sister to compete to get him water. It was much longer that they realised Aamir's trick to get them to work for him.

Aamir was a charmer since his younger days. He would charm all the young girls in the neighbourhood. His old aunts still reminiscent over how Aamir was always surrounded by girls and they would call him 'Krishna Kanhaiya' for attracting so much female attention.

While at school, he formed a band along with his cousin, Nasir Husain's son Mansoor Khan and Aditya Bhattacharya who was grandson of great Bimal Roy and son of Director Basu Bhattacharya.

Even though Aamir was reluctant to face the camera and was confused about her career choices, he was very certain that he wanted to learn the fine nuances of film making by staying behind the camera. After completing his junior college from Narsee Munjee College, Ville Parle, Mumbai, he decided to stop studies and start work.

Aamir's parents were not too keen for Aamir to pursue a career in movies as family had seen many ups and downs in Bollywood and knew how fragile the existence in film world can be. They wanted him to pursue further studies and become a doctor or an engineer. They were not very happy with Aamir's decision to quit studies but Aamir was certain that he wanted to pursue movie making. He asked his father to allow him Film and Training Institute of India (FTII) Pune to study the art of movie making but Tahir Khan refused and asked him to start assisting his uncle, Nasir Hussain as an assistant. He could not study at FTII, Pune but acted in some of the documentaries made at FTII before launching his acting career.

Aamir assisted Nasir Hussain for four years. He was paid one thousand rupees a month as a salary.

Besides working in movies, Aamir also worked backstage with Theatre Group – Avantar. He also played a small role in Gujarati play – *Kesar Bina* at Prithvi Theatre and a small role in an English play *Cleaning House.* On the Bengali version of show *Kaun Banega Crorepati* where he participated with his second wife Kiran Rao – 'Ke Hobe Banglar Kotipoti' in year 2011, he shared the memories from his childhood with the host cricketer Saurav Ganguly and also sang a song that was part of the play.

Paranoia (1983)

In 1983, at the age of 18, he acted and also assisted his friend Aditya Bhattacharya in direction of a 35 minutes silent film called *Paranoia* which had Neena Gupta and Victor Banerjee as his co actors. The movie was funded by actor Sreeram Lagoo who was a friend of Aditya's father Basu Bhattacharya. Unfortunately, prints of this movie is not available in public domain now.

Manzil Manzil (1984), Zabardast (1985)

But Aamir was certain that he wanted to take a shot at film making. He assisted his uncle, Nasir Hussain as assistant director for two of his movies: *Manzil Manzil* (1984) and *Zabardast* (1985). While working behind the camera, he experienced the transitional difference between front of the camera and behind the camera. He experienced tantrums of the actors and mood swings, the challenges faced by the production. His experience as an assistant director helped him in his own grounding and gentle behaviour as an actor during the later part of his life.

Holi (1984)

In 1984, Ketan Mehta signed Aamir for a role of a rebellious college student in a hard hitting coming of age drama *'Holi'* which also starred Ashutosh Gowarikar, Neeraj Vohra, Babloo Mukherjee,

Neeraj Vohra, Kittu Gidwani, Naseeruddin Shah, Om Puri and Deepti Naval. There were no hero or heroine in the movie. The movie was based on the lives and turmoil in the life of students living in a hostel while studying at a college. Most of the actors were students of Film and Television Institute of India, Pune and movie was mainly shot within the premises of FTII. Since it wasn't a commercial movie, it had a limited screens release.

Qayamat Se Qayamat Tak (1988)

Aamir's cousin Mansoor Khan, son of his uncle Nasir Khan had produced a TV serial *Andar Baahar* earlier and also wrote/produced a telefilm *Umberto.* He was ready with script of a feature film *Qayamat Se Qayamat Tak* and wanted to cast new faces as a debutant pair. Aamir was the Assistant Director for the movie and was actively involved in the audition process. Even though behind the camera work interested Aamir, somewhere in his heart, he felt he would like to face the camera too. He had experienced acting in *Paranoia* and *Holi,* another movie *Raakh* was on floor too. He finally asked Mansoor for an audition for the lead role and rest, as we say, is history. Audition was done with two looks, one with moustache as his *Holi* character and the other without moustache which was eventually finalised. Both Mansoor Khan and producer Nasir Khan finalised Aamir for the role.

It is interesting to know here that Aamir also took audition of Juhi Chawla, Ms. India of that year, who also acted with him in many films later on. Juhi did not know Aamir was her hero much after her audition and selection for the role.

Qayamat Se Qayamat Tak had seasoned actors like Dilip Tahil, Beena and Alok Nath in supporting role. It also had Aamir's close friend and future brother-in-law Raj Jutshi in his best friend and cousin's role in the movie. Aamir's brother Faisal Khan did cameo as part of gang of goons who harass Juhi Chawla (Rashmi). The movie was made with two endings, one happy and one sad. It was decided to retain the sad ending. The movie was released in the year 1988.

During the shooting of the movie, Aamir had secretly married his girlfriend Reena Dutta 18 April 1986. Reena Dutta was daughter of a senior Air India official and lived in the Air India building across from Marina building where Aamir stayed with his family. Air India building had many pretty girls and Aamir along with his brother would sit in their balcony which they called *parikhana* (The land of beautiful girls) and look at the girls across the building. Reena Dutta's balcony faced Aamir's and that is where their attraction for each other grew. Loved ensued. Satyajit Bhatkal, Aamir's school friend and director of his TV show Satyamev Jayate, recalls in the book that he wrote on *Lagaan*

"Aamir came from a filmi family that was totally immersed in film culture and Reena came from a household where films were looked down upon and more emphasis was given on studies. Besides that, they belonged to different religion. But they were in love and despite of opposition from both the families, Aamir and Reena got married secretly." The news of their marriage was kept under wraps around the release of the movie but it came out later eventually. In fact, Reena who was visiting Aamir on sets during the shoot of the movie ended up sharing brief screen space with Aamir in the song *"Papa Kehte Hain"*. Post success of *QSQT*, Aamir and Reena moved into a flat gifted by Tahir Khan in the same building where his family lived.

Qayamat Se Qayamat was an instant hit amongst youth. Aamir Khan became a heart throb of millions of women across the country. The soulful singing of Udit Narayan and Alka Yagnik had youngsters crooning the songs, making it a musical success as well. The songs like *'Papa Kehte hain bada naam karega'*, *'Akele hain to kya gam hai'*, *'Gazab ka hai din soho zara'* still sound as melodious and soulful as they did at the time of their release.

Aamir recalls how people would instantly recognise him when he travelled by bus or auto or any public transport. He decided to buy a car. Since he still did not have luxury of money, he bought his first car, Maruti 800 by taking a loan.

Not only *Qayamat Se Qayamat* Tak was declared a commercial hit, earning a huge profit for the producers, it also won award for the best film promoting popular and wholesome entertainment with a Swarna Kamal with ₹ 40,000 presented to M/s Tahir Husain Films and a Swarna Kamal with ₹ 20,000 to director Mansoor Husain Khan for presenting fresh and clean charm on celluloid with discerning imagination at 36th National Film Festival 1989.

At 36th National Film Festival 1989, Aamir Khan was given a citation under special mentions stating "The Jury desires to highlight the imaginative, innovative and promising performance of character roles in *Qayamat Se Qayamat Tak* and *Raakh* by Aamir Khan."

He also won the best debut (Male) award at 1989 Filmfare awards. *'Papa Kehte Hain'* song was nominated for the best male singer award the same year.

In the evenings, after the shooting of the movie, Aamir and his friend, Raj Justshi would go around Bombay, posting posters on the back of autos. Posters asked people to watch out for new faces in *Qayamat Se Qayamat Tak*. In the times of pre-internet and social media, this unique marketing ploy generated enough curiosity around the movie. Therefore, *Qayamat Se Qayamat Tak* turned out to be the debut platform for marketing genius Aamir

Khan who continued to use innovative strategies to promote his movies.

Raakh (1989)

Directed by Aamir's friend Aaditya Bhattacharya, *Raakh* was a tale of revenge against the abuse faced by Aamir's friend Supriya Pathak in the movie. The tagline of the movie was "His Greatest Fight Was For Justice." The movie also starred Pankaj Kapur in a prominent role of a cynical cop who supports him to face the harsh realities of a vigilante life and avenge for the wrong done from the hooligans. The film may not have been a commercial success but it won three critical awards at the 36th National Films Festival 1989 and a Filmfare nomination for Aamir but was restricted to the art film circles and did not find a release. The movie eventually developed a cult following in the years to come.

This film also marked Bollywood debut of cinematographer Santosh Sivan and film editor A. Sreekar Prasad.

With QSQT, a new star had risen on the horizon of somersaulting Hindi Movie Industry.

□

li but it was a box office disaster. Aamir ad said post Dev Saab's death that this was ly movie he had signed without reading pt.

na Mujh Sa Nahi (1990)

eased in 1990, this movie had a grand g but turned out to be a disaster. Aamir nd Madhuri Dixit's pair failed to win the e with this love story but in the same year r delivered the highest grosser of 1990, Indra s *Dil*.

ere Ho (1990)

duction, screenplay and direction of the vas by Aamir's father Tahir Hussain, this ovie had lead pair of *QSQT*, Aamir Khan Chawla and Aamir's brother Faisal Khan Assistant Director in the movie. His sister Khan also helped with costume designing. han was casted as a Snake Charmer but the id not work on the box office and movie create any impression on the audience.

e of these movies were able to recreate c of *Qayamat Se Qayamat Tak*. Some fared nd some had very low box office collection. was not very kind to the outcome of these Some film magazines labelled Aamir as a ovie wonder like Rajendra Kumar's son

Courtesy : Aamir Khan @ Twitter

Courtesy : Google photos

All izz well ... All izz well.

(3 IDIOTS)

3

The Up Swingi
Swinging (Ye

As it is said, success bı
the success of *Qayama*
Aamir Khan had filled the
of a young and sensitive
film industry but the journ
In 1989 and 1990, he sig
had simultaneous release
his pairing with Juhi Ch
typecasted him as the c
Some of these films, ***Love***
Dev Anand's multi starrer
Mujh Sa Nahi and *Jawani*
on the box office.

Awwal Number (1990)

Released in 1990, the
Dev Anand. The movie
The movie also starred

Pancho
Khan h
the on
the scri

Deewa

Rel
opening
Khan a
audienc
this pai
Kumar'

Tum M

Pro
movie v
1990 m
and Juh
was an
Nusrat
Aamir K
charm d
failed to

Non
the magi
average a
Industry
movies.
single m

Kumar Gaurav. Then, came the movie *Dil* that changed the game for Aamir once again and proved to be a career saviour for him.

Dil (1990)

In June 1990, a movie directed by Indra Kumar and starring Madhuri Dixit as his co-star bought back the box office success that had eluded Aamir Khan in last one year. *Dil* was a romantic drama and Aamir Khan had Anupam Kher, Saeed Jaffri and Sarita Joshi as his co-stars in the movie. The music was by Milind Soman and it had chart buster songs such as *'O Priya Priya'*, *'Mujhe Neend Na Aaaye'*.

Aamir was not very convinced about playing the character of carefree Raja as he feared this character may typecast him in a certain role like his previous movies but then his secretary convinced him to take the role.

The movie found a connect with youngsters and was the highest grosser of the year 1990. Madhuri Dixit earned her first Filmfare award for the best actress for this movie in the year 1990. The movie was remade in Telugu in year 1993 as *Tholi Muddhu* and starred Late Divya Bharati and Prashanth. It was remade in Bengali in 1996 as *Amaar Ghar Amaar Behesto*.

Launch of Andaaz Apna Apna (1990)

Producer Vinay Kumar Sinha and Director

Rajkumar Santoshi had the launch party of their new movie *Andaaz Apna Apna* at Sun n Sand Hotel in Bombay in October 1990. The star cast for this comic caper was Aamir Khan, Salman Khan and debutant Raveena Tondon and Karishma Kapoor. The Muhoorat Shot was given by veteran actor Dharmendra. Aamir's friend and cricketer Sachin Tendulkar also attended the launch party along with other big names from Bollywood. Somehow, shooting of the movie was stalled for another three years due to packed work schedule of the star cast. It was Aamir who bought together the star cast and the movie was released in April 1994.

Afsaana Pyaar Ka (1991)

Afsaana Pyaar Ka was a love story between Raj (Aamir Khan) and Nikita (Neelam Kothari) whose families are in conflict with each other but they are oblivious to the animosity brewing between their families. They meet in college, fall in love and decide to elope after family's opposition. The film did average on the box office but a song from the movie *'Tip Tip Baarish'* became a sensational hit.

Dil Hai Ki Maanta Nahin (1991)

Director Mahesh Bhatt casted Aamir Khan in the unofficial adaptation of 1934 Hollywood Classic *It Happened One Night* along with daughter Pooja Bhatt who was debuting in her first adult female lead role. *It Happened One Night* was remade as *Chori Chori* earlier, starring Raj Kapoor and Nargis. The musical romantic drama *Dil Hai Ki Maanta Nahin* was produced by Gulshan Kumar. It also had Anupam Kher, Tiku Sultania, Avtar Gill, Javed Khan etc. in important supporting cast. The movie was an instant hit with the audience and all twelve songs were liked by the movie watchers.

Isi Ka Naam Zindagi (1992)

The movie *Isi Ka Naam Zindagi* had Faraz Naaz with Aamir as the lead pair and a strong supporting cast of Pran, Shakti Kapoor and Asrani. The movie was set in Pre Independence British Era and had a plot of land as subject of dispute. Despite of having a strong support cast, the movie was a disaster on the box office.

Daulat Ki Jung (1992)

Daulat Ki Jung, a 1992 movie also had lead pair of QSQT, Aamir Khan and Juhi Chawla and it is one of those rare films which spelled tragedy at box office for the super hit pair. It also had Paresh Rawal and Kader Khan in the supporting roles.

Year 1992 was a decisive year in the career of Aamir Khan. Reflecting upon the hits and misses on box office in his short movie career of four years, he realised that he had made some wrong choices and hasty decision in selecting the movies in last two to three years. ***He decided to concentrate on one or two movies every year and pay special emphasis on the script and director. This strategy was a great milestone in the career of Aamir Khan and some of his most iconic and successful movies followed in next 23 years.*** Having stated that, failure was not futile for Aamir. As he quoted in an interview many years later:

"I have had many unsuccessful films but I learnt a lot from these films. I give my failures as much importance as my success."

Jo Jeeta Wohi Sikander (1992)

Jo Jeeta Wohi Sikander was a coming of age story of a recluse and good for nothing school student Sanjay Lal Malhotra (Aamir Khan) who prove his mettle in the end and emerges out as a district cycle race champion. The movie is said to be inspired from 1979 American Movie *Breaking Away*.

The movie was directed by Mansoor Khan and co-starred Ayesha Jhulka, Mamik Singh, Deepak Tijori and Kabir Bedi's daughter Pooja Bedi. The movie grossed INR 728 million at the box office. It earned Jatin-Lalit a nomination for Filmfare Best Music Director Award. Movie was remade in Bengali as *Champion*, Telugu as *Thammudu* and Tamil as *Badri*.

The film also had Amol Gupte in a cameo as a commentator during the cycle match. Aamir Khan and Amol Gupte collaborated for *Taare Zameen Par* after few years.

Hum Hain Rahi Pyar Ke (1993)

Hum Hain Rahi Pyar Ke was produced by Aamir's father Tahir Hussain and directed by Mahesh Bhatt. Aamir Khan co-starred with Juhi Chawla, Sharokh Bharucha and Kunal Khemu (as a child artiste) in this movie. The film was remake of Hollywood movie named *Houseboat*. Aamir also co-wrote the screenplay of the movie along with Robin Bhatt.

The film won: Filmfare Best Film Award

Juhi Chawla won Filmfare Best Actress Award

Filmfare Best Lyricist Award to Sameer

National Film Award for best female playback singer to Alka Yagnik

National Special Jury Award for Mahesh Bhatt

It was also nominated for:

Filmfare Best Director Award for Mahesh Bhatt

Filmfare Best Actor Award for Aamir Khan

Filmfare Best Music Director Award for Nadeem-Shravan

Filmfare Award for Best Female Playback Singer– Alka Yagnik

Pehla Nasha (1993)

This 1993 movie was directorial debut of

Aamir's friend Ashutosh Gowariker. A remake of Brian De Palmas 1984 thriller *Body Double.* Deepak Tijori played the lead role with Pooja Bhatt, Raveena Tandon and Paresh Rawal. The film also has cameo appearances by Aamir Khan, Shahrukh Khan, Juhi Chawla and Saif Ali Khan as themselves. It is the only film to feature Aamir Khan and Shahrukh Khan in a scene together. Ashutosh Gowariker recently commented that it may also be the last time the two actors share screen space together. Other upcoming actors at the time such as Sudesh Berry and Rahul Roy also appeared in the same scene. Upon release, the film received poor reviews and failed at the box office.

Parampara (1993)

Parampara is a 1993 Hindi movie starring Aamir Khan,. Sunil Dutt, Vinod Khanna, Ashwini Bhave, Ramya Krishna, Saif Ali Khan, Raveena Tandon, Neelam Kothari and Anupam Kher. The film is produced by Firoz A. Nadiadwala and directed by Yash Chopra. His son Aditya Chopra wrote the screenplay for the film. The film was also launch pad for Saif Ali Khan. The film was slammed by the critics for a weak storyline, average music and bad direction by Yash Chopra. It was a commercial flop. The movie was shot in the famous Indian boarding school Mayo College.

Damini (Cameo 1993)

Aamir Khan appeared in a song along with Meenakshi Seshadri in the movie *Damini* which was directed by his *Andaz Apna Apna* Director Rajkumar Santoshi. According to the story that song required a star hero. Aamir Khan gave the cameo appearance as himself in the movie. The song had classical dance movements. Dressed in traditional white kurta pyjama, Aamir perfectly matched steps with Classical trained dancer Meenakshi Seshadri.

Andaz Apna Apna (1994)

Listed at ***Number 30 of IMDb Cult Classics*** you cannot miss, *Andaz Apna Apna* remains the only movie where Aamir Khan and Salman Khan acted together as two good for nothing young men Amar and Prem who want to woo and marry daughter of man NRI billionaire. The film turned out to be a cult classic in years to follow and remains as one of the most cherished films of Aamir Khan. A Hindi comedy film directed by Rajkumar Santoshi starring Aamir Khan, Salman Khan, Raveena Tandon, Karishma Kapoor and Paresh Rawal in leading roles that released on 4 November 1994. Juhi Chawla, Mehmood had cameo roles in the movie. Even though The movie recovered cost as it did average business in big cities but over the years, it emerged as a ***cult***

classic film and remains a personal favourite of Aamir Khan himself, in fact he played a catalyst to ensure that this movie is completed despite of delays. The film was nominated for the 40th Filmfare Awards in four categories: Best Film (Producer – Vinay Kumar Sinha), Best Director (Rajkumar Santoshi), Best Actor (Aamir Khan) and Best Comedian (Shakti Kapoor) who played Crime Master Gogo.

The character of the movie needs special mention here as some characters turn out to be classic hits. On completion of 25 years of *Andaz Apna Apna* in Year 2014, Aamir Khan wore a T-shirt with logo and photo saying "Save Crime Master Gogo" to honour the cult movie.

What Makes Andaz Apna Apna A Cult Film?

Wikipedia defines a cult film, also commonly referred to as a cult classic, as a film that has acquired a cult following. Cult films are known for their dedicated, passionate fanbase, an elaborate subculture that engage in repeated viewings, quoting dialogue, and audience participation.

1. Cult films are known for their dedicated fanbase: *Andaz Apna Apna* didn't do well at box-office, it recovered its cost mainly due to business from big cities, but didn't turn out to be a massive hit contrary to everyone's expectations. The major reason of the film was way ahead of its time and mid-90s was not a time for start to finish full comedy movies that involves no emotion, no drama or no seriousness at all.

2. An elaborate subculture that engages in repeated viewings: In subsequent years, it has achieved a cult classic status among Indian Hindi audiences. On the video circuit and TV, it has become one of the most popular Indian movies over the years.

3. Quotable dialogues: Each dialogue and character of the movie are immensely likeable and have terrific recall. Such is the cult following of this movie that many people have memorized the dialogues of this movie like "Teja main hu. Mark Idhar hai", "Crime Master Gogo, Mogambo ka Bhatija", etc.

Rangeela (1995)

> *"Ramu had four flops. Urmila had eight. Film had no story but I decided to play the role of the Underdog."*
>
> **—Aamir Khan**

The risk taker in Aamir decided to believe his gut feel and agreed to play the role of Munna, an underdog who secretly loves Mili, a dancer and aspiring actress.

Rangeela was the first rustic character played by Aamir Khan on the screen. It followed with another similar character in movie *Ghulam*. It was a big gamble for Aamir as both Urmila and Ram Gopal Varma had series of flops before this movie was conceived. Aamir's character was rustic and had shades of insecurity, jealousy, helplessness and awareness of his limitations. It was probably the multi dimensionality of the character that made Aamir pick up the role of Munna in *Rangeela*. The movie was a hit and rest, as the say is history.

Directed by Ram Gopal Varma and Aamir Khan co-starred with Jackie Shroff, Urmila Matondkar, Gulshan Grover and Avtar Gill. Film collected INR 210 million at box office and became the fourth highest grosser of 1995. Music of the movie was by A.R. Rehman and it gave hit songs as "Aayi Re, Aayi Re", "Tanha Tanha" and "Rangeela Re" in meliflouos voice of Asha Bonsle. Ram Gopal Varma received Filmfare Best Story Award for the film.

The film received critical acclaim and won seven Filmfare awards that year. They were:

Best actor in supporting role – Jackie Shroff
Best choreography – Ahmed Khan
Best Costume Designing – Manish Malhotra
Best Story – Ram Gopal Varma
Best Music – A.R. Rahman
The RD Burman Award – Mehboob
Special Jury Award to Asha Bhosle

Baazi (1995)

Film was directed by Ashutosh Gowariker and Aamir Khan co-starred with Mamta Kulkarni, Paresh Rawal and Avtar Gill. The film collected INR 92.5 million at box office and declared as a moderate hit.

Baazi is a 1995 Indian action film directed by Ashutosh Gowariker and starred Aamir Khan and Mamta Kulkarni. Aamir played the role of a police inspector, Amar Damji. This film laid the base for Aamir Khan's selection as the determined police officer in the blockbuster *Sarfarosh* which turned out to be one of Aamir Khan's best performances. He again played role of a police man in Reema Katgi's *Tallish* in year 2011.

Aamir performed an item number *"Doley Doley Dil Doley"* in disguise of a glamorous woman and to add authentic also waxed body hair to look like a woman. Another example of sincerity of Mr. Perfectionist.

Aatank Hee Aatank (1995)

Aatank Hee Aatank is a 1995 crime drama written, edited and directed by Dilip Shankar. The movie is highly inspired by *The Godfather*. It starred Rajnikanth, Aamir Khan, Juhi Chawla and Archana Joglekar in the lead. In 2000, the film was dubbed into Tamil as *Aandavan*.

Aamir the Perfectionist

For a sequence in the song "Aakha Hai Bombai", Aamir Khan was to play the 'dafli'. While the unit broke for lunch, Aamir Khan walked up to the choreographer, and requested the choreographer to let him practice playing the 'dafli', to get the correct beat, and not look uncomfortable on screen. He skipped lunch, and practiced through the lunch break, and finally, when the sequence was shot, he gave a perfect shot.

The honest and professional Aamir once apologised profusely for coming late on set saying he had overslept.

Akele Tum Akele Hum (1995)

Produced by Ratan Jain of Venus Films and directed by Mansoor Khan, this was the third and last film Aamir Khan acted under direction of his cousin who stopped making movies after *Akele Tum Akele Hum*. The film was written by Mansoor Khan and Nasir Hussain (Dialogues). It starred Aamir Khan along with Manish Koirala and master Adil. The movie was released in 1995 and did average business at the box office despite of a decent storyline and good acting by the lead pair. The plot of the movie was based on 1979 Academy winning film *Kramer Vs. Kramer* starring Meryl Streep and Dustin Hoffman.

Raja Hindustani (1996)

Raja Hindustani was directed by Dharmesh Darshan and Aamir co-starred with Karishma Kapoor, Rajwinder Deol, Suresh Oberoi, Navneet Nishan and Johnny Lever. The film was made with modest budget of INR 50 million and grossed INR 2078.8 million at box office. It was declared to be a super hit. Karisma Kapoor won Filmfare Best Actress Award and Aamir Khan won Filmfare Best Actor Award. The film created a controversial because of a long kissing scene in the movie.

Ishq (1997)

Ishq a 1997 comedy drama film was directed by Indra Kumar and Aamir Khan co-starred with Ajay Devgan, Juhi Chawla, Kajol, and Shweta Menon. It was the most expensive Bollywood film ever made in Bollywood of that time. The film was declared a hit and grossed INR 300 millions at box office. The movie was remade in Kannada as *Snehana Preethina* starring with Darshan, Aaditya Sindhu Tolani and Lakshmi Rai.

Ghulam (1998)

Ghulam is a 1998 Indian action crime drama film directed by Vikram Bhatt and starring Aamir Khan and Rani Mukherjee. The film was inspired by Elia Khajan's 1954 movie, *On the Waterfront*. *Ghulam* did moderately well at the box office and was declared as 'SuperHit'. *Ghulam* also debuted Aamir as a singer when he sung hit sing "*Aati kya Khandala*" in the movie.

1947: Earth (1998)

Based on Pakistani writer Bapsi Sidhwa's book *The Ice Candy Man,* Aamir played a complex character with grey shades in the movie *1947: Earth* as Dil Nawaz, the ice candy man who loves the maid of the Affluent Parsi household and turns negative to pursue his unrequited love. Set around the time of India Pakistan partition, this period drama was directed by Deepa Mehta and had Nandita Das, Kittu Gidwani, Rahul Khanna, Arif Zakaria and Maia Sethna. *Earth* is the second instalment of Mehta's Element Trilogy. It was preceded by *Fire* (1996) and followed by *Water* (2005). It was India's entry for the Academy Award for Best Foreign language Film. The story is set in Lahore in the time period directly before and during the partition of India in 1947.

Sarfarosh (1999)

Sarfarosh was written, produced and directed by debuntant director John Matthew Matthan and Aamir Khan co-starred with Sonali Bendre, Mukesh Rishi, Naseeruddin Shah, Govind Namdeo, Makrand Deshpande and Shri Vallabh Vyas. The film grossed INR 180 million at the box office, becoming the seventh highest grosser of the year. The movie also coincided with Kargil war between India and Pakistan and the patriotic tone of the movie connected with the current sentiments of the audience. The film was remade in Kannada and Telugu. Aamir Khan received nomination for Filmfare Best Actor Award.

The movie also had some catchy and soulful songs such as *"Hosh waalon ko khabar kya"* and *"Jo haal dil ka"*.

Mann (1999)

The *film* was directed by Indra Kumar and co-starred Manisha Koilara, Sharmila Tagore, Anil Kapoor, Rani Mukherjee and Neeraj Vora. Movie is a remake of old classic *Bheegi Raat* (1965) starring Ashok Kumar, Meena Kumari and Pradeep Kumar, and is also a frame-by-frame copy of 1957 Hollywood classic movie *An Affair to Remember.* The film grossed INR 21 crore at box office and was declared a hit. The film was remade in Telugu as *Ravoyi Chandamama* starring Akkineni Nagarjuna, Keerthi Reddy and Anjala Zhaveri.

Mela (2000)

Mela is a 2000 action masala film directed by *Raja Hindustani* director, Dharmesh Darshan. It starred Aamir Khan his brother Faisal Khan and Twinkle Khanna. It is still remembered for being one of the biggest box-office failures of the year 2000. The rustic village Sholasque setting did not go well with audience. This film was an attempt by Aamir to revive his brother's film career as a hero. Faisal was launched earlier in *Madhosh* by Tahir Khan but the movie had failed. Recently, during her book *Mrs. Funnybones* release, now columnist and writer, Twinkle Khanna accepted that *Mela* made her realise what a terrible actress that she was and she decided to quit her film career thereof. Faisal Khan suffered some health issues including Schizophernia in the following years but is ready now for a re-launch in a movie based in Kashmir, called *Chinar: Daastaan-E-Ishq* is based on Urdu novel *Jheel Jalti Hai* by former bureaucrat-turned-politician Farooq Ahmad Renzu.

□

Courtesy : *Aamir Khan @ Twitter*

Courtesy : Google photos

Vishvas aur ghamand mein bahut kum farak hai … main kar sakta hoon, ye mera vishvas hai … sirf main hi kar sakta hoon, yeh mera ghamand.....

(GHAZINI)

4

Year 2001–Year 2016

Year 2001–Birth of Aamir Khan Productions with Lagaan

A.K. Productions Pvt. Ltd. is a reflective and risen over the ground establishment that started its journey with 2011 movie *Lagaan*.

When Ashutosh Gowariker initially shared the script of *lagaan* with Aamir Khan, Aamir was very sceptical with the pretext of he movie. But Ashutosh improvised upon the script and managed to get Aamir to produce *Lagaan*. Aamir roped in finance Jhamu Sughand to finance the movie. Aamir's then wife Reena Dutta was the executive producer who managed production of the mammoth production with help of Aamir's sister Nikhat and executive producer B. Srinivas Rao.

Lagaan: Once upon in India (2001)

The film was directed by Ashutosh Gowariker and Aamir Khan co-starred with Gracy Singh, Rachel Shelley and Paul Blackthorne. The film was made with budget of INR 250 millions and grossed INR 578 millions at box office. *Lagaan* is the third Indian film nominated for Academy Award for Best Foreign Language Film. *Lagaan* won eight National Awards and nine Filmfare Awards.

Captain Russell: Tum Bolo...Haar gaye toh.... doogna lagaan Dogey. Sharat manzoor hai....

Bhuvan (Aamir): Sharat manzoor hai....

Lagaan is a story of determination, teamwork and self- belief – the movie reiterates that once one has vowed to face and fight against all odds with total conviction, nothing is impossible.

Costumes were done by celebrated costume designer Bhanu Atthaiya who ensured the authenticity in dressing of each character of this period drama.

Lagaan met with high critical acclaim and both critics and masses loved the verve of the movie.

Making of Lagaan

Aamir was very certain from the beginning. Only those who had faith in the project should come on the board. It was all about guts.

This is an excerpt from the book *Making of Lagaan*:

"The film had a start to finish schedule in a single schedule during which each member of the unit was living their character in *Lagaan*. Every department of this film, be it music, location, costumes, background music, songs, etc. had attempted nothing short of perfection to show that characters are living their own story. Local people helped. The main challenge was to create facilities for hundreds of people arriving from Mumbai and far away England. In Bhuj, far away from the location, Sahajanand Towers was redone to suit the metro crowd and their lifestyles. Near about sixty rooms were created, with air conditioners and proper sanitation facilities. The royal challenge was shooting in the dry environs of Kutch; the location does not support human habitation. It was difficult to create a village existing in times of the British Raj in such place. Every morning before the break of dawn the entire cast and crew had to assemble in the bus which would take them to the location. The team together faced several challenges and overcame them."

The film entered the syllabus of IIM Indore as a case study. Many companies conducted workshops to learn how to handle human resources. Today *Lagaan* is a success story on and off the screen. It was **India's Nomination at 74th Academy Award (Oscars) in year 2012** under Best Foreign Film Category and it reached the top 5 even if it could not win the award. It won the National Award for best film. Aamir Khan won best actor award at Filmfare awards.

Aamir's first director Ketan Mehta commented after watching the movie, "I just saw *Lagaan* and I think Aamir has seasoned as an actor and I'd say he has balls of steel as a producer. I think it's a very courageous venture to invest so much of himself in – not in terms of money, but I'm sure it required a certain grave decision and I'm glad it was a courageous decision rather than a market-driven tame decision."

Amitabh Bachchan exclaimed, "The film is a piece of perfection—I've seen it a number of times already and not because I've done the voiceover but because I've enjoyed it so much.

Dil Chahta Hai (2001)

"Waise bhi perfection ko improve karna thoda mushkil hota hai"

(As it is, it is difficult to improvise upon perfection).

Says Aamir's character Aakash cheekily in the movie, resonating the towering standards Aamir has set for himself in life.

Dil Chahta Hai, the first male bonding movie of 2000 was produced by Ritesh Sidhwani and written/directed by Javed Akhtar's son Farhan Akhtar. Aamir Khan co-starred with Saif Ali Khan and Akshaye Khanna, Preity Zinta, Sonali Kulkarni and Dimple Kapadia in this movie. It was made with budget of INR 140 millions and grossed INR 910 millions at box office. Aamir Khan won Filmfare Best Actor Award and Akshaye Khanna won Best Supporting Actor Award.

Set in modern-day urban Mumbai and partly shot in Sidney, movie focuses on a major period of transition in the lives of three young friends.

In 2001, the film won National Award for Best Feature Film in Hindi.

It performed better in the urban areas of the country compared to the rural areas, which was attributed by critics to the city-oriented lifestyle depicted in which all the characters are from rich or upper-middle-class families. Over the years, it has attained a cult status and also features in the IMDb list of Hindi cult movies.

Career Break

Post *Dil Chahta Hai,* Aamir took a break of four years from film making citing personal problems. By end of 2001, he and his wife Reena Dutta had separated and they filed for divorce citing temperamental differences as reason for mutually-consented divorce after 15 years of marriage.Reena got the custody of the children with visitation rights for Aamir along with access to spend holidays with them. Aamir had met his future wife, Kiran Rao briefly on the sets of *Lagaan* where she was an Assistant Director. He met her again in 2004 during Coke commercial shooting where she was the first AD. There, he got to know her better. After a courtship period, Kiran moved in with Aamir and after living together for one and a half years, they tied knot in year December 2005. After Kiran suffered some miscarriages, they decided to have a child through surrogacy. On 5th December 2011, a son was born to Aamir and Kiran. They named him Azad Rao Khan, named after Shri Abdul Kalam Azad, the freedom fighter and great-grand uncle of Aamir Khan.

Madness in the Desert (Documentary on Lagaan 2004)

Madness in the Desert was made by Aamir's friend Satyajit Bhatkal on the behind the scenes story of making of *Lagaan*. He had also written a book on the making of Lagaan. The documentary went on to win the National Award for Best Exploration/ National Film.

Mangal Pandey (2005)

Mangal Pandey: The Rising (Indian title) or *The Rising: Ballad of Mangal Pandey* (international title) is a 2005 Indian historical film based on the life of Mangal Pandey, an Indian soldier who is known for his role in the Indian Mutiny of 1857. It is directed by Ketan Mehta, produced by Bobby Bedi, and with a screenplay by Farukkh Dhondy. This movie marked the comeback of Aamir Khan who took a sabbatical after release of *Dil Chahta Hai* in 2001. The film was declared 'a hit', even though it took a decent start at the box office but the collections dipped eventually. The film was premiered in the Marche′ du Film section of the 2005 Cannes Film Festival.

Aamir Khan plays the lead role of Mangal Pandey who was a Sepoy whose actions helped spark the Indian Rebellion of 1857. The rebellion is also known as "The First War of Indian Independence."

About Aamir's acting nuances, a fan states on the questioning online knowledge sharing site Quora:

"Aamir is the king of underplay. If you are not careful, you would miss many of his acting cues and mistake him for an ordinary actor. Often we assume loudness of voice, display of intensity and forcefulness of emotions to be signs of great actor. Aamir generally shies away from such common theatrics. Consider this scene:

A scene appears in the movie *Mangal Pandey* where Mangal Pandey comes across a butcher house for cows which inspires him to cause the 1857 revolt. If you are a casual observer, you would watch Aamir standing in the butcher house doing practically nothing. However, if you really 'see' the scene, you would notice the slight twinge of his nostrils. The rancid odor from butcher house is displayed by Aamir in a very, very subtle way. **This is what makes Aamir one of the greatest actors of Indian cinema."**

Rang De Basanti (2006)

Rang De Basanti was produced and directed by Rakeysh Omprakash Mehra and Aamir co-starred with Siddharth Narayan, Sharman Joshi, Waheeda Rehman, R. Madhavan, Atul Kulkarni, Alice Patten, Kiran Kher and Soha Ali Khan. The film, shot in and around Delhi was made with budget of INR 250 million and collected INR 925 million.

The movie won Filmfare Best Movie Awards, Rakeysh Omprakash Mehra won Filmfare Best Director Award. At the time of film release the movie was opposed by Animal Welfare Board as it used a banned Indian horse race.

Upon release, the film broke all opening box office records in India. It was the highest-grossing film in its opening weekend in India and had the highest opening day collections for a Bollywood film. The film was well received and praised for strong screenplay and dialogues.

The story is about a British documentary filmmaker who is determined to make a film on Indian freedom fighters based on diary entries by her grandfather, a former officer of the British Indian Army. Upon arriving in India, she does screening and asks a group of five young men to act in her film.

Rang De Basanti's release faced stiff resistance from the Indian Defence Ministry and the Animal Welfare Board due to parts that depicted the use of MiG 21 fighter aircraft and a banned Indian horse race.

The film was released globally on 26 January 2006 on the Republic Day of India and received critical acclaim winning National Award for most popular film and it is also rated as 8.6 out of 10 on IMDB which is one of the highest among Bollywood films.

It was subsequently nominated for Best Foreign Language Film at the 2006 BAFTA Awards. *Rang De Basanti* was chosen as India's official entry for the Golden Globe Awards and the Academy Awards in the Best Foreign Language Film category, though it did not ultimately yield a nomination for either award. A.R. Rahman's sound track had two of its tracks considered for the Academy Award nomination. The film was well received by critics and audiences for its production values and had a noticeable influence on Indian society. In India, *Rang De Basanti* did well at many of the Bollywood awards ceremonies, including a win for Best Movie at the Filmfare Awards.

Rakeysh Mehra took seven years to research and develop the story, including three to write the script. While some raised doubts about his morale following the failure of his last film, *Aks* at the box office, he retorted by saying that it would not affect him at all. He added that not only did his storytelling technique improve, but past mistakes had helped him improve his filmmaking abilities.

Aamir Khan agreed to act in *Rang De Basanti* immediately after reading Mehra's script. Mehra described his character as a simple man with a strong sense of integrity and dignity. Aamir turned 40 during the shoot, lost about 10 kilograms (22 lb) with a strict diet and exercise regime to more convincingly depict a man in his late twenties. Something that he used reversely for the upcoming movie *Dangal* now where he gained weight upto 100 kgs for the new role of a wrestler.

Fanaa (2006)

The film was written and directed by Kunal Kohli and produced by Yashraj films. Aamir starred with Kajol, Kiron Kher, Rishi Kapoor, Sharat Saxena and Tabu. Kajol played role of a blind girl in the film. It was made with budget of INR 500 millions and earned INR 1.0414 billion at box office. At the release the film was initially banned in Gujarat state for Aamir Khan's criticism about Gujarati government over the Narmada Dam issue.

The film was a critical and commercial success, with many critics opining that the film worked largely due to the performances and chemistry of the leads.

The music of *Fanaa* was composed by Jatin Lalit with lyrics penned by Prasoon Joshi. Five songs are featured in the movie while the soundtrack contains seven songs. This was the last movie for which Jatin Lalit composed as a duo as they split afterwards. The film won major awards.

Taare Zameen Par (2007)

It was directorial debut of Aamir Khan and co-starred Darsheel Safary, Tisca Chopra, Vipin Sharma and Tanay Chheda. The film was about Indian School systems and about the boy with dyslexic. Film was made with budget of INR 120 million and grossed INR 881 millions at box office. The film won Filmfare Best Film Award.

Taare Zameen Par

"Har bachche ki apni khoobhi hoti hai, apni kaabiliyat hoti hai, apni chahat hoti hai..."

—Taare Zameen Par

Taare Zameen Par explores the life and imagination of a dyslexic eight year-old child. The movie was an eye-opener for all parents who force their children to run in the rat race of daily life. In doing this the parents tend to forget that each child has a special ability; Nikumbh becomes pied piper for the little, depressed and different Ishaan leading him to a blissful end.

Ghajini (2008)

Film was directed by A.R. Murugadoss and co-starred Asin, Late Jiah Khan, Pradeep Rawat and Riyaz Khan. The film was remake of Tamil movie *Ghajini* starring Suriya, Asin, Nayantara and Pradeep Rawat. The film was inspired by Hollywood film *Memento*.

The film was made with budget of INR 450 million and collected INR 1.9 billion at box office. *Ghajini* marked Bollywood debut of Asin and she won Filmfare Best Female Debut Award for the movie.

It is a 2008 Indian psychological thriller film written and directed by A.R. Murugadoss and produced by Allu Arvind and Madhu Mantena. The soundtrack and score is by A.R. Rahman. It is a remake of Murugadoss's own 2005 Tamil film starring Surya Sivakumar in the lead role along with Asin and it became the highest grossing movie of that year and the first Hindi film to cross the ₹ 100 crore mark.

On release it became the highest grossing movie of all time until it was beaten by another Aamir Khan movie *3 Idiots* the following year. *Ghajini*'s paid preview collections only were ₹ 27 million (US$ 410,000). Asin made her debut in Bollywood with *Gajini*.

Jaane Tu...Ya Jaane Na (As Producer, 2008)

Aamir Khan launched his nephew Imran Khan with this 2008 romantic love story *Jaane Tu...Ya Jaane Na*. Written and directed by Abbas Tyrewala, the film stars Genelia D'Souza and Imran Khan in pivotal roles. Produced by Mansoor Khan, Aamir Khan, it marks the directional debut of Abbas Tyrewala, the debut of Imran Khan (Aamir Khan's nephew) and Prateik Babbar as actors, and the re-appearance of D'Souza in Hindi cinema. Released on 4 July 2008, the film received positive reviews, and went on to become a super hit at the box office. The music was by A.R. Rahman.

3 Idiots (2009)

It was directed by Rajkumar Hirani and co-starred Kareena Kapoor, R. Madhavan, Sharman Joshi, Boman Irani and Omi Vaidya. The film was made with budget of INR 35 crore and earned INR 392 crore at box office, becoming one among the highest grossing Bollywood film. It was remade in Tamil as *Nanban* starring Vijay, Jiiva, Srikant and Ileana D'Cruz. *3 Idiots* won Filmfare Best Film Award and Filmfare Best Director Award.

> *"Jab bhi darr lagey – Dil pe haath rakho aur bolo all izz Well."*
>
> **—3 Idiots**

3 Idiots was an eye opener for the whole education system in India. It raised questioned against conservative and rigid Indian curriculum and futility of it. The quest to acquire a degree rather than knowledge was ridiculed and movie encouraged the youngsters to follow their hearts and dreams, do what makes them happy and cultivate it to their best potential.

Luck By Chance (Cameo 2009)

Luck by Chance is a 2009 Indian drama film written and directed by Javed Akhtar's daughter Zoya Akhtar. Produced by Farhan Akhtar and Ritesh Sidhwani, it stars Farhan Akhtar and Konkona Sen Sharma in the lead roles. Many stars and industry folk starred as themselves like Aamir Khan in seamless cameos.

Peepli Live (As Producer, 2010)

A 2010 satirical comedy film, *Peepli Live* exposed the apathy shown towards 'farmer suicides' and the subsequent media and political circus to gain TRP and mileage respectively from the tragedy. Written and directed by Delhi -based Anusha Rizvi in her directorial debut and produced by Aamir Khan Productions, the film received critical appreciation. Naya Theatre company's member Omkar Das Manipuri along with Naseeruddin Shah, Raghbir Yadav, Nawazuddin Siddiqui, Malaika Shenoy and Shalini Vatsa acted in the movie.

Peepli Live was also India's official entry for the 83rd Academy Awards Best Foreign Film category but did not get a nomination.

Movies like *Lagaan* and *Peepli Live* bought out

socially conscious persona of Aamir Khan who connects with grave issues of rural India despite of living in a metropolitan city all his life.

Delhi Belly (As Producer, 2011)

Delhi Belly is a 2011 Indian Black Comedy film written by Akshat Verma and directed by Abhinay Deo. It starred Aamir Khan's nephew Imran Khan, Kunaal Roy Kapur, Vir Das, Poorna Jagannathan and Shenaz Treasurywala. While the original version was in English, a Hindi-dubbed version was also released. The film is produced by Aamir Khan Productions and IBC Motion Pictures. The theatrical trailer of the film premiered with Aamir Khan's *Dhobi Ghat* on 21 January 2011 while the film was released on 1 July 2011. The film was given an 'A' Certificate for the profane language and sexual content. The film was remade in Tamil as *Settai*.

The film was banned in Nepal initially due to profanity and sexual content but was cleared later.

Dhobi Ghat (Producer and Actor, 2011)

Dhobi Ghat (also known as *Mumbai Diaries*) is a 2011 Indian drama film directed by Kiran Rao in her directorial debut. The film produced by Aamir Khan Productions, Reliance Entertainment, Shree Ashtavinayak Cine Vision Ltd. starred Aamir Khan along with Prateik Babbar, Monica Dogra, Kriti Malhotra and Kittu Gidwani in lead roles. Gustavo

Santaolalla was signed to compose the score and soundtrack of the film, which includes a song by Ryuichi Sakamoto.

Dhobi Ghat had its world premiere in September 2010 at the Toronto International Film Festival and was released on 21 January 2011 in cinemas. The film being mainly tagged an Art and Parallel cinema was critically successful, as it well received and appreciated by critics. The film was long listed for 65th BAFTA Awards for Film Not in the English Language category. In a press conference, director Kiran Rao mentioned *Dhobi Ghat* is a tribute to Bollywood superstar Salman Khan. The lead actor Prateik Babbar plays a Salman Khan fan in the movie. The film was a *Below Average* grosser at the box-office.

Aamir's character was as reticent, artistic and sensitive as Aamir in his real life.

BIG IN BOLLY WOOD (Documentary, 2011)

Aamir did a cameo in the documentary.

27-year-old American-born Omi Vaidya, a struggling actor in L.A., miraculously lands a dream role in the Bollywood film *3 Idiots*. Curious to better understand the world of Bollywood, four of Omi's buddies armed with cameras fly to Mumbai to document his big premiere. Within a week of release, *3 Idiots* skyrockets to box office success, becoming the most successful Indian film in history and transforming Omi into an overnight megastar. But being a national sensation in India is not all glitz and glamour. Aside from the language barrier, Omi struggles with the pressure of his newly-acquired fame and continuing his career momentum while trying to maintain a healthy domestic life back in Los Angeles. Set against the backdrop of Mumbai, *Big in Bollywood* is a film about what it is to be successful in show business, seen through the eyes of Omi's best friends, who witness his career transformation first hand.

TV SHOW – SATYAMEV JAYATE (Launched on 6 May 2012)

In 2011, during the Bengali Version of KBC show, *Ke Hobe Banglar Kotipoti*, cricketer and show host Saurav Ganguly asked Aamir, "Your contemporaries; like Hritik Roshan, Salman Khan and veteran artiste like Sh. Amitabh Bachchan are all doing TV shows, why have you not ventured into TV?"

Aamir replied that if he want to come of television with a program, he would like to come with a program that has connect with every human being's life and gets him closer to the heart of India.

And he did make a show within a year, under his production house Aamir Khan Productions Limited. Under the direction of Aamir's friend

Satyajit Bhatkal, on 6 May 2012, *Satyamev Jayate* was launched on Star Plus with a simultaneous telecast on Doordarshan for wider reach to the far away interiors in India who do not have the luxury of satellite cable. 11 am every Sunday became the mandatory Satyamev Jayate hour for the families to huddle together and see Aamir talking to the panel of guests and audiences in the studios, visiting faraway places in the country to highlight the pertinent issues plaguing our society such as dowry, female foeticide, homosexuality, elder abuse, water woes, lack of education, etc.

A team of over 100 people including team for Star Plus worked on making of Satyamev Jayate. Some names are as follows:

Director: Satyajit Bhatkal

Producers: Aamir Khan, Kiran Rao

Co-Director and Field Research Head: Svati Chakravarty Bhatkal

Core Creative Team: Aamir Khan, Satyajit Bhatkal, Svati Chakravarty Bhatkal, Monika Shergill, Lancy Fernandes, Manisha Mudgal, Suresh Bhatia, Christopher Rego

Music Composed, Arranged and Produced by: Ram Sampath

Associate Producer: B. Shrinivas Rao

Research Head: Lancy Fernandes

Associate Director: Suresh Bhatia

Director of Photography: Baba Azmi

Online Director: Arun Sheshkumar
Production Designer: T.P. Abid
Online Editor: Dongrej Gor
Audio Engineer: Cheerag Cama
Senior Creative Associates: Christopher Rego, Prerana Thakurdesai, Ritu Bharadwaj

Satyamev Jayate not just created awareness about the various issues but also talked about a possible resolution with persistent follow up.

Aamir's warm eyes convey a thousand emotions. He is as stubborn as he is sensitive, a replica of his mother. There's a great force in his steady gaze. "A number of the topics on Satyamev Jayate were related to women–domestic violence, female foeticide, dowry, honour killings. Though we may want to tag these as women's issues, let's face it, the problem lies with men. Women suffer because men take away their right to choose: the right to choose the way they want to live, love and dream. The problem is that we don't just not empower woman, we willfully dis-empower them. We do not want the girl child to be born. And if she survives, we make sure that she knows she is not important enough. At every level – nutrition, health, education – we gave her a raw deal. The sad part is that a lot of women also buy into this patriarchal thinking. They endorse it, and the cycle continues."

Aamir admits that one of life's most profound lessons was taught to him by a woman. "I used to play competitive tennis at the state level when I was in my teens. One day, I won a significant match, arid, as always, when I came home I saw my mother eagerly waiting at the door to find out the result. When I told her that I had won, she hugged me joyously. Later in the day, while I was still basking quietly in my success, she came up to me and said, 'Beta, you know the boy who lost against you today...I wonder what his mother feels like right now.' I was stunned into silence, for I had not seen my victory from that perspective. My mother was not trying to teach me anything that day, but, as usual, she taught me much with the way she led her life. I like to think that my sensitivity, my ability to feel what the other person is feeling is something that I have imbibed from her."

Aamir said that *Satyamev Jayate* is a personal journey of self-realisation. It means understanding issues that are close to all of us. I personally believe that I am responsible as anybody else for the way things are. *Satyamev Jayate* is not about moral policing. Many times, we don't even show individuals' faces. For us, it is not about an individual, but about trying to find a way forward. I believe that with knowledge and information we can change our actions and attitude. That is the essence of *Satyamev Jayate*.

All we wanted to bring out was the truth, with complete honesty. It a live audience; at the end of the day, every recording goes differently, and viewers have strong opinions of their own. The transformation was not simply in the viewers, it was in us too.

Aamir Khan's hugely successful TV show *Satyamev Jayate*, that focuses on burning issues facing India and ways of tackling them, has landed him on the cover of prestigious *Time* magazine as India's "first superstar-activist."

Tracing the rise of Aamir Khan with the 1988 blockbuster hit *Qayamat Se Qayamat Tak*, *Time*'s Bobby Ghosh noted over the past decade the 47-year-old actor has acted in, directed and produced a string of "movies that artfully straddle the demands of popular cinema and that desire for grace."

"Now, with his groundbreaking TV show *Satyamev Jayate* (Truth Alone Prevails), he has dispensed with commercial considerations to indulge his conscience," writes Ghosh. "With it, Khan has taken on the mantle of the country's first superstar-activist."

"The show, in equal parts chat and journalism, casts an unblinking spotlight on some of India's ugliest social problems," he says of the show of which Khan is "creator, producer and host, and he has invested it with his star power – and his credibility."

"It's a ballsy move, and potentially jeopardizes his status as the beloved idol of millions," writes

Ghosh, since the subjects his show tackles "are precisely the sorts of harsh realities from which many of Khan's fans seek escape in his movies."

"Can a movie star affect the mores of a nation of 1.2 billion?" asks Ghosh and suggests "It might just be possible in India, where a national obsession with cinema, unparalleled in the world, gives popular actors an influence beyond the imagination of Hollywood scriptwriters."

As Khan assesses the impact of his first series, *Time* suggests, "Whatever Khan chooses to do next in his quest for grace, there's a good chance it will lift India a little closer to what he – and fellow Indians – would wish their country and society to be."

Aamir Khan is the third Indian actor to be featured on the cover of *Time* magazine. Aishwarya Rai made it to the cover in 2003 and Parveen Babi was featured in 1976.

TALAASH (2012)

Talaash: The Answer Lies Within is a 2012 Indian neo noir pschological thriller film directed by Reema Kagti. It was produced by Excel Entertainment and Aamir Khan Productions. The movie starred Aamir Khan with Kareena Kapoor Khan, Rani Mukherjee, Nawazuddin Siddiqui and Shernaz Patel. *Talaash* was made with budget of INR 400 million and collected INR 1.74 billion at box office. Rani Mukherjee won Filmfare Best Actress Award for supporting role. The soundtrack of the movie is scored by Ram Sampath with lyrics written by Javed Akhtar. Principal photography of the film took place during March-November 2011, primarily in Mumbai, Pondicherry and London. With a UA Certificate from Censor Board of India, the movie released on 30 November 2012. Declared a semi-hit, *Talaash* eventually grossed ₹ 1.36 billion (US$ 21 million) worldwide.

DHOOM 3 (2013)

Aamir termed his role of twins Samar and Sahir in *Dhoom* as the most challenging role of his career.

Made under Yashraj Films banner, *Dhoom 3* was written/directed by Vijay Krishna Acharya and produced by Aaditya Chopra. In the third instalment of *Dhoom* series, Aamir's co-stars in the movie were Katrina Kaif, Abhishek Bachchan, Uday Chopra and Jackie Shroff. *Dhoom: 3* was made with high budget of INR 1.25 billion and was extensively shot in Mumbai, Chicago and other parts of US with elaborate bike chase. The climax of the movie was shot in Switzerland. Made on a budget of ₹ 175 crore (US$ 26 Mn), it became most expensive Indian films of all time and collected INR 5.42 billion at box office, becoming the highest grossing Indian film of all time but was superseded by another Aamir Khan movie, *PK* in year 2014-15.

Though the movie was panned by critics for its peak story line, it broke many records on its opening days in India and abroad. Box office of India declared *Dhoom 3* "the biggest hit of 2013" after two days of release. The film went on to gross ₹ 4 billion (US$ 60 million) worldwide in just ten days, to become the highest grossing Bollywood film of all time in international markets. The initial international gross of *Dhoom 3* was US$ 28 million eventually breaking the record of *3 Idiots* (another Aamir movie) and making it the third highest grossing Bollywood film of all time in international markets as well as the fourth highest grossing Indian film of all time. It was the 77th highest grossing film of 2013 worldwide.

The film was screened during the 2014 International Film Festival of India in the *Celebrating Dance in Indian cinema* section.

SATYAMEV JAYATE (Season 2, 2014)

Aamir Khan's **talk** show *Satyamev Jayate* returned for another season in 2014 and its second innings started with a bang. The first episode focussed on the epidemic of 'violence against women' that has gripped the nation since the horrific Delhi gangrape incident of December 16, 2012.

The second episode was about 'police'. The police are insensitive and sometimes brutal towards the public. This has instilled fear in our hearts and minds. But what has made the police this way? In this episode, we look at the problems that the police face and examine solutions for reform offered by officials and experts. Until we reform the police, we cannot bring out change in our society.

The third episode was on "Don't waste your garbage." Imagine taking a walk or going for a drive in your neighbourhood and seeing a beautiful tree or a bed of flowers in areas where we now see mounds of garbage. This can become a reality. All we have to do is to start adopting eco-friendly solutions to treat the thousands of tonnes of garbage we generate every day, instead of holding our noses and turning away like we do now. There are methods available that are cost effective and easy to implement. This episode looks at these solutions as well as the people who are trying to make a difference, in ways big and small, across India. It is time we started listening to them if we want to tackle the environmental and health risks posed by the garbage that is just piling up every day.

The fourth episode talked about 'Kings Everyday'. Just walking down to your polling booth and casting a vote does not make for a successful, vibrant democracy. For that citizens need to engage on a regular basis with the government system. Eternal vigilance is the price of democracy and every citizen has a duty to monitor its workings. However, we have all become armchair critics – content to sit back and criticize the establishment. Instead, let's find ways to play a more active role and collectively take charge of our governance.

The fifth episode tackled the issue of 'Criminalization of Politics'. It is the issue under focus in the final episode of Season 2. Through facts and figures, and the lived experiences of officials and activists working in the field of governance, the many ways in which our democracy has been undermined down the decades is highlighted. The episode emphasises that we, the people of India, have a duty to cast our vote in the Lok Sabha elections in an informed, ethical manner, and not sell our vote, our self-respect.

The episodes talked about fighting rape, police, garbage and hygiene conditions, corruption and ended with a bang giving its take on the importance of voting. With the Lok Sabha polls round the corner, the finale episode Aamir Khan talked about the importance of casting the vote, electoral reforms, the good and bad in politics among others. In the episode, the maker urged the people to make an informed decision.

Satyamev Jayate tweeted, "Cast your vote,

don't vote your caste. Make an informed choice in the 2014 elections. #MyVoteNotForSale." Even as the episode was being aired, celebrities and others took to Twitter to highlight how the finale episode of 'Satyamev Jayate 2' is a 'must watch'.

PK (2014)

PK is a 2014 Indian Satirical Science Fiction Comedy movie directed by Rajkumar Hirani, produced by Hirani and Vidhu Vinod Chopra, written by Hirani and Abhijit Joshi, the film stars Aamir Khan in the title role with Sanjay Dutt, Anushka Sharma, Sushant Singh Rajput, Boman Irani, Saurabh Shukla in supporting roles. It is story of an alien who comes to Earth on a research mission. He befriends a television journalist and questions religious dogmas and superstitions.

The film received positive reviews and emerged as the HIGHEST GROSSING INDIAN FILM OF ALL TIMES and ranks as the 70th highest grossing film of 2014 worldwide. *PK* was the first Indian film to gross INR 7 billion worldwide. It was also the first Indian film to gross US$ 100 Million (₹ 630 crore) worldwide.

SATYAMEV JAYATE (Season 3, 2015)

Satyamev Jayate revamped for the third season. A series of videos with the tagline '*#Mumkin hai*' were released to give a glimpse of what to expect including a personal selfie video by Aamir citing a Dushyant Kumar's sher:

"Kaun Kehta hai aasmaan mein chhed nahi ho sakta.

Ek patthar toh tabeeyat se ucchaalon yaaron."

(Who says the sky cannot be penetrated, throw up a stone with all your heart, my friends).

The trailers, presented in the show's documentary style, feature real interviews with people who have been affected by the show, on a deeper, personal level.

Celebrity Interaction

New feature added. "There was some celebrities on the show this time. Topstars from the industry for some episodes. "They were there on the show not because they are celebrities but they are related to the issue...they will be contributing for the show," shared Aamir Khan told the media.

Live Interaction

"This time I will be live with the people. We can get opinion and suggestion of people immediately. I will also connect with them through Twitter and Facebook. So this is a new element in our show," the 49-year-old actor-host said.

Duration

Each episode in the third season of *Satyamev*

Jayate was set to be of two hours and thirty minutes long. The extra hour will be reserved for "directly interacting with the audiences."

The season premiered on September 21 had six episodes in the season.

The trailers released by the makers of *Satyamev Jayate* showed the story of women who have been victims of domestic violence.

The next video showed a former alcoholic, who under the influence of alcohol, would beat up his wife and children. "I saw the number on screen one day, and simply decided to call. The best part was, the person on the other side actually picked up the phone and talked to me warmly," says the man.

Another video shared the horrifying tale of child abuse. One little girl saves other little girl in her village, with the help of the helpline numbers shown during the show.

DIL DHADAKNE DO (2015)

Written by Reema Kagti and Zoya Akhtar, Directed by Zoya Akhtar, Aamir played the voice of family dog of Mehra family whose life made the base of *Dil Dhadhakne Do.* Zoya wanted someone to have a philosophical yet observant narrator of the movie based on a cruise who can bring the satire and humour in the narration. Aamir Khan was a perfect choice. Its a role that Aamir enjoyed rendering his voice to.

In fact, Reema and Zoya showed the initial rushes of movie to Aamir for his critique and feedback. Says Zoya, "We consult Aamir with our initial work. He is a great friend, gives honest and precise feedback with a no nonsensical approach and also does not talk about it to others."

Dil Dhadakne Do received good response and was declared a hit.

DangAl (In Making, 2015-16)

Aamir's latest movie Dangal again proved his sensitivity and how he handles a delicate social issue with lot of gentle care. So, it does not hurt anybody and touches the hearts of millions.

Success of the film Dangal shows how effectively any message can be conveyed by the film to the society. Dangal is like a rainbow of emotions. It blends lot of emotions, various shades of a person and society, sportsmanship and patriotism extraordinarily has been shown in this movie. If I start explaining each and every scene which has a hidden message, this chapter will never come to an end.

But, of course, would like to draw attention on few sequences how beautifully they put a message. Not only the film scenes, even dialogues just nourish your senses including correct emotions, music is in terrific sync with the mood of the film and lyrics of songs are also very apt and carry the message.

Title track – begining line – "Maa ke pet se Marghat Tak hai Teri Kahani Dangal – Dangal" – shows how life every moment throws a challenge towards you. However, dealing with is all about life.

How beautifully it sums up the whole life in a few lines! Life is full of pleasures and worries. No matter what dark life offers you, there is always a ray of hope. The only thing is we have to identify. Like in movie, when the hero wanted to pursue his dreams, he wanted a boy and never think that a girl also can pursue his dream. It shows the fixed mindset of society, which is so strongly imbibed in our system that we blindly set boundaries for boys and girls.

We don't treat them as individuals. Of course, there is a physical difference, but it hardly affects one mentally and emotionally.

The story of Dangal shows the zest of life that the children should bear faith of their parents and parents too should have faith on their children's capability. If you believe yourself, nobody can stop you to touch your dreams.

Dangal adds another milestone contribution in the Indian cinema regarding broaching up a social issue in a very entertaining and inspirational manner. The film has several messages. Dangal is a masterpiece– a terrific film that stays in your heart and remains attached in your memory much after the screening has concluded. It will be remembered as a classic in times to come.

From the beginning, when a father decided that his girl will do wrestling, what kind of odd situations he had faced from his own family members and society? Even girls were also not ready to do. In a sense, where girls curse their father in front of their friend who is getting married, then that girl's emotional words about her feelings towards their caring father is very cute, emotional and enough to make girls realise what they are taking for granted.

Dangal is not just a movie. It is an experience to be cherished and every scene of their movie is woven so practically and emotionally that everyone can relate one's self in some or the other way. A very simple scene, where a protagonist massages the feet of his sleeping daughter, clearly reflects that he is not just a ruthless coach but a caring father too.

Climax of the film comes with a strong message for the sport as well as for life that one can train you but only you have to implement the techniques which make you true winners and enriches-self confidence. "Tumhare papa hamesha tumhare sath nai rahenge." This dialogue adds very important colour in the painting of parenting, through which it would not complete. Inspite of giving all teaching, we should teach our children to take a stand and believe in ownself.

□

Courtesy : Aamir Khan @ Twitter

Courtesy : Google photos

Zindagi jeene ke do hi tareeke hote hain ... ek jo ho raha hai hone do, bardaasht karte jao ... ya phir zimmedari uthao use badalne ki.

(RANG DE BASANTI)

5

Aamir Khan's Cinema and Social Issues

Introduction

Indian cinema has had a long and illustrious run, even more than a century. In this century-long journey of twists and turns, there have been a few actors who have really made a lasting impact on the Indian society as a whole – one of them is Aamir Khan. After an initial start as the quintessential *loverboy*, Aamir Khan took measures to make movies having a social bearing as well. In this last decade of Indian cinema's century, Aamir Khan has left an indelible mark on the pages of Indian cinematic history. A lot of Aamir Khan's movies have significant social and societal undertones; they revolve around social issues and show the face of contemporary Indian society.

For the purpose of my research, three movies have been chosen to demonstrate the qualitative correlation (not the research technique) between

Aamir Khan's movies and their social impacts. These three movies are of three different genres and they cover almost all of the different sections of the society, which is what merits their selection. The three movies taken for the aforementioned purpose are – Lagaan, 3 Idiots and Taare Zameen Par.

Lagaan

> *"Hamaar pasina hamre tann mein khoon ban ke daudega"*
>
> —**Lagaan: Once Upon a Time in India**

Story of Lagaan

Lagaan is a story of self-esteem, determination, teamwork and, more importantly, belief in oneself – the movie demonstrates the belied that when one is prepared to face and fight against all odds with total conviction, nothing is impossible.

Lagaan is set in the Victorian period of India's colonial British Raj. The story revolves around a small village Champaner, where the villagers lived under the oppressive rule of the "tribute" system in the British Raj, where their king was but a dummy and exercised no real power at all and they had to pay high taxes. When the villagers find themselves in a very difficult situation, an arrogant British officer challenges them to a game of cricket as a wager to avoid the taxes.

Under the "tribute" system, the king had to pay a certain portion of his earnings to the Britishers for protection of sovereignty. In order to maximise the earnings, the kings usually levied different taxes on agricultural produces. The scenario was that due to successive years of droughts, the farmer-villagers of Champaner were barely able to harvest enough crops for sustenance and, therefore, were not able to pay taxes. Villagers went to Raja Puram Singh (king of Champaner territory) to ask for a waiver of the taxes, but despite his intention to do so, he is unable to help them as he is also bound by the British law. When the villagers went to officials, they were busy in playing cricket and villagers had to wait till the end of the game. During this period, Bhuvan, the hot-headed youngster of the village (played by Aamir Khan), mocks at the game and gets into a skirmish with one of the British officers. Taking an instant dislike to Bhuvan, Russell offers to waive the taxes for three years if the villagers can beat his men in a game of cricket. The catch, however, was that if the villagers lost, however, they would have to pay three times the amount of their normal taxes. Bhuvan accepts this challenge on behalf of all the villagers, without their consent. As can be expected, there is an outrage at Bhuvan's reckless move.

Gradually gathering support from the villager, Bhuvan begins to prepare the villagers for the match. In his efforts, Elizabeth (played by Rachel Shelley), the soft-hearted, fair sister of Capt. Russell joins to support Bhuvan and his band of rebels. Eventually, as the villagers realise that winning will give them an unprecedented opportunity to gain freedom, and as a few of them are insulted by the British, most of them either join the team or come in its support. Gradually, after a lot of turbulent moments, Bhuvan succeeds in making a team of his own to take on the British contingent.

The second half of the film focusses on the match itself, which is spread over a period of three days. On the first day, Russell wins the toss and elects to bat, giving the British officers a strong start. Bhuvan brings Kachra into the match only to find that Kachra, the untouchable (played by Aditya Lakhia) has somehow lost his ability to spin the ball, because new cricket balls do not spin as well as worn-down ones (like the team had been practising with). In addition, as part of his agreement with Russell, Lakha deliberately drops many catches. During the evening, however, Elizabeth sees Lakha (played by Yashpal Sharma) meeting with her brother. She races to the village and informs Bhuvan of Lakha's deception. Rather than allow the villagers to kill him, Bhuvan offers Lakha the chance to redeem himself.

The second day of the match was even more dramatic as the day brought redemption for the Champaner side. At this point, however, the

British have already amassed a huge total, losing only three wickets by the lunch break. Kachra is brought back to bowl. Bowling with an old ball, Kachra takes a hat-trick which sparks the collapse of the British batting side. The villagers soon start their innings. The British side took advantage of the inexperience of the Champaner side with their brutal bowling and continuous sledging; attempts were made on each and every player of the home side. The villagers' team ends the day with 4 batsmen out of action with barely a third of the required runs on board.

On the third and final day, Bhuvan passes his century, while most of the later wickets fall. The Champaner side struggled a lot, but limping (some of the members, quite literally), the team reached to the ultimate over of the game. With one ball remaining and the team down 5 runs, Kachra knocks the ball a short distance, managing only a single. However, the umpire signals a no-ball and Bhuvan returns to bat, and swings extremely hard at the next ball. Captain Russell back pedals and catches the ball, gleefully believing that the British team has won, until he realises that he actually caught the ball beyond the boundary. The final signal of the umpire was 6 runs, and the win went to Bhuvan's team. Even as they celebrate the victory, the drought ends as downpour occurs.

Primarily, the fact is that the film revolves

around Bhuvan. The film is about how Bhuvan, just one of the villagers, accepts a challenge, how he faced initial opposition to everybody, how he managed to convince everybody to take up this challenge and many more things. But, at the same time, the film is not just about him. It is about so many other things as well. It is about the problems and the hurdles that the whole village came across, how they solved all problems and eventually won the fight of pride and honour. It is about how they face the arduous task of learning a semi-alien game and playing for a result that would change their village's destiny.

Lagaan shows various shades of human life, behaviour and emotions. It shows an innate sense of empowerment and shows that in hope lies an individual's greatest strength. Lagaan showed not just India, but the world that the Hindi film industry is capable of making a movie with high production values and a strong script. The film had no special effects or complex editing, but it had a story of universal human value. Lagaan shows self-esteem, integrity, unity, strength, discipline, fighting spirit, inspiration, love, equality, determination and a lot many other things. Lagaan shows that true hope never dies.

The songs of Lagaan are an added dimension to the movie experience on the whole. The songs are melodious, but more importantly, they are also about Indian morals and values. Almost all the songs of the movie are inspiring in a way and have a great impact on the viewers of all demographic groups. Lagaan, not just through its songs, but also through the screenplay, shows the purity of feeling called love.

Lagaan was met with high critical acclaim. Roger Ebert, the legendary international movie critic, said, "Lagaan is an enormously entertaining movie, like nothing we've ever seen before, and yet completely familiar.... At the same time, it is a memory of the films we all grew upon, with clearly defined villains and heroes, a romantic triangle, and even a comic character who saves the day. Lagaan is a well-crafted, hugely entertaining epic that has the spice of a foreign culture."

Sudhish Kamath of THE HINDU suggested, "The movie is not just a story. It is an experience. An experience of watching something that puts life into you, something that puts a cheer on your face, however depressed you might be."

John Nugent of the Trenton independent, who wrote "A masterpiece... and what better way to learn a bit about India's colonial experience. History and great entertainment, all rolled into one (albeit long) classic film."

Social Issues emerging out of Lagaan

There are several issues that Lagaan as a

movie highlights, which were relevant to both the prevalent social schema of the country at that point in time and the freedom struggle against imperial rule. Following are some of the more prominent ones:

1. **National Integrity:** Lagaan very dramatically and beautifully shows the unity and national integrity. The portrayal of the grief-stricken villagers, as depicted by the characters who make a team, was what made the movie so special. The movie is one of the perfect examples which show how the devil actually lies in the details. For instance, the team has a Hindu player Bhuvan, a Muslim player Ismail, a Sikh player Deva, people from the then lower classes – Lakha, Kachra and Arjan, all coming together to fight against the British Raj.
2. **Injustice:** Injustice is intolerable at any cost. People should fight against injustice in a very positive manner. In the words of renowned American writer, Edward Abbey, "A patriot must always be ready to defend his country against its government." Lagaan depicts how Britishers did injustice to people and how people found the courage within them to take a stand against such injustice.

3. **Untouchability:** When the team needed one more player, when they were ready to settle for anyone, it was then that Bhuvan found his teammate in an untouchable, Kachra, who could bowl spin. The villagers, conditioned by the traditional prejudice against untouchables, refused to play if Kachra joined the team. Bhuvan chastises the villagers shaming them into accepting Kachra.

It is a well-known fact that there is a multitude of social issues prevalent in the society. But the important point to note is that the movie also emphasises the role of youth in changing the face of a society.

The Making of Lagaan

The positive impact of Lagaan is pretty well known and has been described amply earlier as well. But, few are privy to show behind the making of Lagaan. It is fairly obvious that the team behind Lagaan must have put in a lot of dedication, teamwork, hard work and focus.

The entire film was to be shot from start to finish in a single schedule during which each and every member of the unit was living the world of Lagaan. Every department of this film, be it music, location, costumes, background music, songs, etc., had attempted nothing short of perfection to show that characters are living their own story. Creating an entire village with people required the help of the local people. Nearly sixty actors to play members of the families were selected from Mumbai and Kutch. However, one of the biggest challenges was to create facilities for hundreds of people arriving from Mumbai and far-away England. In Bhuj, far away from the location, Sahajanand Towers was redone to suit the metro crowd and their lifestyles. Near about sixty rooms were created, with air conditioners and proper sanitation facilities. The royal challenge was shooting in the dry environs of Kutch; the location does not support human habitation. To create a village existing in times of the British Raj became all the more difficult in such a place. Every morning, before the break of dawn, the entire cast and crew had to assemble in the bus, which would take them to the location. The team together faced several challenges and bravely overcame them during its filming.

The film entered the syllabus of IIM Indore as a case study. Many companies conducted workshops to learn how to handle human resources. Today, Lagaan is a success story on and off the screen. Aamir's first director Ketan Mehta commented after watching the movie, 'I just saw Lagaan and I think Aamir has seasoned as an actor and I'd say he has balls of steel as a producer. I think it's a very courageous venture to invest so much of himself in—not in terms of money, but I'm sure it required a certain grave decision and I'm glad it was a courageous decision rather than a market-driven tame decision." Amitabh Bachchan exclaimed, "The film is a piece of perfection—I've seen it a number of times already and not because I've done the voice-over but because I've enjoyed it so much."

Primary Data Findings

The survey, which was conducted in the age group of 18-25, primarily reveals two things – the message and impact of the film on the society and the creation of social awareness by the film.

Message and impact of the film on the society

India is one of the youngest populaces in the world. The youth of this country has emerged as a strong change driver. They seek inspiration from a lot of many things; one of them is films. Lagaan, having a very strong social backbone, sends a message to the youth on different notes.

Key message gained through Lagaan

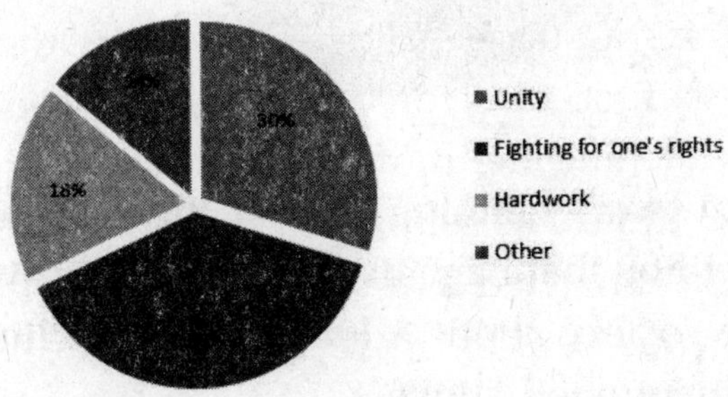

A careful analysis of the data gathered clearly suggests the most important message that the film sends is that one should fight for his/her own rights. Many times, a society, or atleast a section of it, finds itself in a situation where the rights are in jeopardy. It is at this time that the denizens of the society, especially the younger ones, must rise and fight for their rights and that of their fellow countrymen. This is the strongest message that Lagaan sends. 30% of the respondents also consider unity as one of the most important messages that Lagaan depicts. They are of the belief that without the entire team functioning as a single, cohesive unit, the victory could never have been achieved.

Does Lagaan create social awareness ?

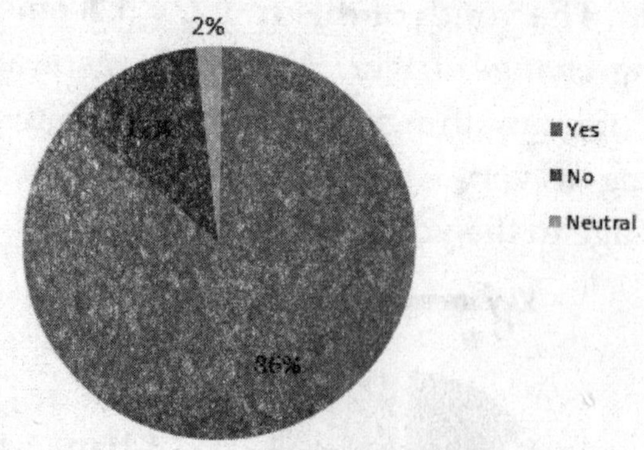

An overwhelming 86% of the sample was of the opinion that Lagaan creates positive awareness in the society about a lot of issues including the ones mentioned above.

Observations about Lagaan

Lagaan, an iconic film, had a great impact on Indian cinema. It was a lesson to the film industry that a story which appeared to be so simple when handled with skill and love could create magic. This magic touched the very core of the audience. The fire of the young farmer Bhuvan and his ambition to raise himself and his villagers from the drudgery of the British was awe-inspiring. His determination in the face of opposition filled the audience with similar determination to face their problems and never give up to injustice. The nail-biting end brings relief to everyone and the hero not only wins the game but also his lady love.

3 Idiots

"Bachcha kabil bano, kabil... Kamyabi toh jhak maar ke peeche aayegi."

Story of 3 Idiots

3 Idiots, simply put, is a story of 3 friends who represent today's youth and how they tackle our education system. In this movie, Farhan Qureshi (played by R. Madhavan), Raju Rastogi (played by Sharman Joshi) and Ranchhoddas Chanchad "Rancho" (played by Aamir Khan) are students at the Imperial College of Engineering, one of the premier colleges in India. The dean of this college, Professor Viru Sahastrabuddhe a.k.a. Virus (played by Boman Irani) is very strict and

a follower of orthodox educational system rules. When new students join the ICE, Virus is shown to call them and tell them about the fountain pen invented so that people can write in space. It is here that Rancho makes an entry, asking Virus that if normal pens didn't work in space, why they didn't use a pencil instead.

3 Idiots then shows these 3 students and how they face problems, how they handle the pressure of marks, exams and make way towards their dreams. Their story is framed as intermittent flashbacks from the present day, which is ten years henceforth from their college lives, in which Raju and Farhan are in search of Rancho. They are joined by Chatur (played by Omi Vaidya), now a wealthy businessman, looking to seal a deal with scientist Phunsukh Wangdu. At the house ascribed to Rancho, they discover another individual (Jaaved Jaffrey) under that name, whom they blackmail by seizing his father's ashes and threatening to flush them down a toilet. Thus threatened, the householder reveals that their friend was an orphan servant boy who loved learning, while he himself disliked it. Therefore, the family sent the servant to study in his master's place, until graduation, where after the master pockets the qualifications and the benefits thereof, while the impersonator becomes a school teacher in Ladakh.

Raju and Farhan then take Pia (played by

Kareena Kapoor) to Ladakh, where they see inventions resembling those of their friend. When the latter's friends ask his real name, he identifies himself as Phunsukh Wangdu, Chatur's prospective business partner. Upon learning this, Chatur is horrified and begs Phunsukh to establish the business relationship, apparently to no effect.

3 Idiots went on to become one of the highest grossers of the Indian film industry. It is a fun-filled, entertaining film cocktailed with social messages. For instance, one of the most important aspects of human life discussed in the film is "self-actualization". One of the primary reasons behind 3 Idiots' success is that although it widely entertained people, it was equally provocative, funny and insightful at the same time. All these factors fascinated the audiences repeatedly to the theatres. The film questioned the present education system, which, in a misguided effort to enhance the performance of students, was perhaps curtailing their innate intelligence and common sense. The good part is that while the film raised several questions, it also provided answers through the characters in a way which was understandable and appealing to all classes of the society. The film did not talk about winning at all costs. Instead it gave hope to people that if one loves to do something, following it would make him/her happy and, therefore, positively lead to success.

One of the most important messages for students was the pursuit of excellence over success. The film was made with lot of substance, thus having a strong impact on the viewer. People can still be found assuring themselves with the phrase "Aal Izz Well" (the message was put through a song in the movie).

Critical Reception of 3 Idiots

Subhash K. Jha, a renowned film critic and author of 'The Essential Guide to Bollywood', states, "It's not that 3 Idiots is a flawless work of art. But, it is vital, inspiring and life-revising work of contemporary art with some heart imbued into every part. In a country where students are driven to suicide by their impossible curriculum, 3 Idiots provides hope. Maybe cinema can't save lives. But, cinema, sure as hell can make you feel life is worth living. 3 Idiots does just that, and much more. The director takes the definition of entertainment into directions of social comment without assuming that he knows best."

Nikhat Kazmi of The Times of India suggests, "The film is a laugh riot, despite being high on fundas." Mayank Shekhar of The Hindustan Times comments, "This is the sort of movie you'll take home with a mile and a song on your lips." According to Taran Adarsh of Bollywood Hungama, "3 Idiots – it's emotional, it's entertaining, it's enlightening. The film has tremendous youth appeal and feel-good factor to work in a big way."

Derek Elley of Variety wrote that "3 Idiots takes to while to lay out its game plan but pays off emotionally in its second half." Robert Abele of Los Angeles Times wrote that there's an "unavoidable joi de vivre (symbolised by Rancho's meditative mantra "All is Well") and a performance charm that make this one of the more naturally gregarious Bollywood imports." Louis Proyect described it as a "fabulous achievement across the board. A typical Bollywood confection but also social commentary on a dysfunctional engineering school system that pressures huge numbers of students into suicide".

Primary Data Findings on 3 Idiots

In consort with the survey conducted, the findings are indicative of two trends – the message conveyed by the movie and the creation of social awareness.

Key message delivered by 3 Idiots

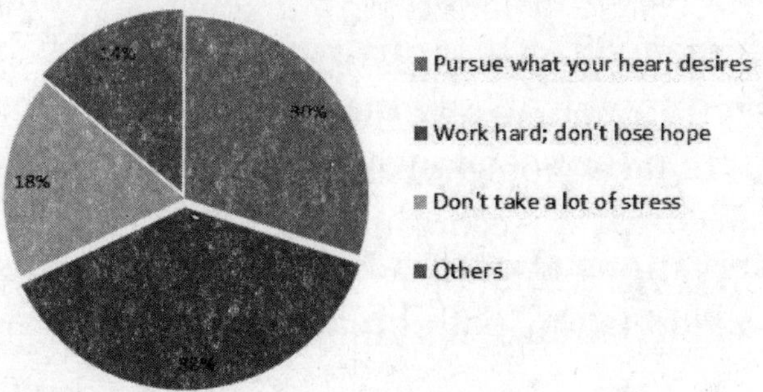

Although there was a bevy of messages conveyed through the film, the maximum importance perceived was that of persistence. The youth of this country, as depicted by the sample, is of the opinion that the core message that 3 Idiots gives is that there will always be failures in the journey towards success; the important thing is to continue on that road. Another important stimulus of the movie was that an individual, especially a student, should pursue something s/he is passionate about.

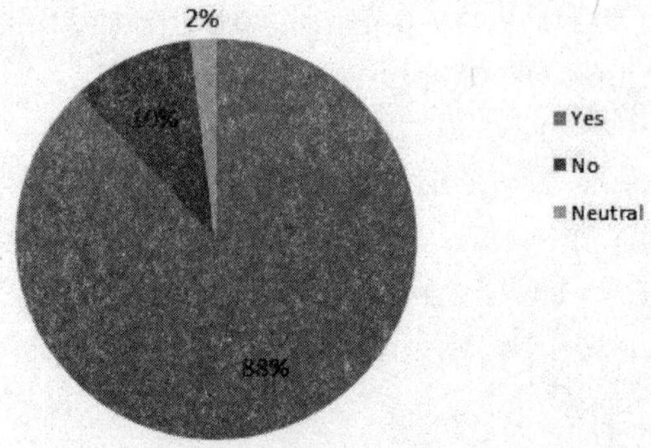

As far as the creation of social awareness is concerned, 88% (marginally higher than Lagaan) of the respondents say that 3 Idiots has a positive impact on the social awareness in the society.

Observations about 3 Idiots

3 Idiots, a path-breaking movie, was an

eye-opener for the whole education system in India. It questioned the conservatively established Indian curricula, rising and flourishing since quite some time. The competition to acquire a degree rather than knowledge was and is always preferred.

When Rancho chose knowledge over degree, he felt and believed in his gut that what he did was absolutely right. The film depicts his belief to have come true when, towards the end, he signs a contract with the dean's prized pen. The question that still remains to be answered is that although such things are possible in the Western countries, has India as a country graduated to that level to make such dreams come true?

Taare Zameen Par

> *"Har bachche ki apni khoobi hoti hai, apni kabiliyat hoti hai, apni chahat hoti hai..."*
>
> **—Taare Zameen Par**

Story of Taare Zameen Par

The film starts with a scene where Ishaan Nandkishore Awasthi (played by Darsheel Safary) catches a fish from a local pond using his socks and captures it in his water-bottle; suddenly, the school bus conductor comes and scolds him that because of his carelessness, the whole bus had to wait for quite some time. This scene, in a nutshell, is the summation of the problems that Ishaan faces. The child is not doing anything wrong; he is an epitome of innocence. However, it also shows that this small boy has his own world and he is completely engrossed in it.

The movie is a story about Ishaan Nandkishore Awasthi, an eight year-old boy, who dislikes school and fails every test or exam. He finds all subjects difficult, and is scolded by his teachers and parents alike. But Ishaan's internal world is rich with wonders, something which he is unable to convey to others. The kid had an artist inside him, waiting to be unleashed in front of the world. Ishaan's father, Nandkishore Awasthi (played by Vipin Sharma) is a successful executive but a strict person, who expects his children to excel. Consequently, he imposes such discipline on both of his children. Ishaan's mother, housewife Maya Awasthi (played by Tisca Chopra) is frustrated by her inability to educate her son. Ishaan's elder brother, Yohan (played by Sachet Engineer) is an all-round scholar and Ishaan faces constant comparison with him.

After receiving a poor academic report, Ishaan's parents decided to send him to a boarding school. He declined to go but they sent him and tell him that he got punishment. It is there that Ishaan hit his personal nadir. He sinks into a state of fear and depression, despite being befriended by Rajan Damodaran (played by Tanay Chheda), physically disabled and one of the top students in the class. Ishaan's situation changes when a new teacher, Ram Shankar Nikumbh (played by Aamir Khan), joins the school as a temporary instructor. An instructor at the Tulips school for young children with developmental disabilities, Nikumbh's teaching style is different from that of the previous strict teachers. He quickly observes that Ishaan is unhappy and contributes little to class activities. On inquiring about Ishaan to his friend Rajan, he comes to know that Ishaan has some problems but nobody knows what he actually feels. On reviewing Ishaan's classwork, he concludes that Ishaan's academic shortcomings are indicative of dyslexia.

On his day off, Nikumbh visits Ishaan's parents and asks if he can see more of their son's work. He is stunned by the sophistication of one of Ishaan's paintings, and tells his parents that Ishaan is a bright child who processes information differently from other children in his class, but Ishaan's father is suspicious that the explanation is simply an excuse for his son's poor performance. Nikumbh describes dyslexia to them and explains that it is not a sign of low intelligence. He tells them he can provide extra tutoring that will help Ishaan, highlighting the boy's artistic ability evident in his many paintings and other creative works. In a particular class, as the students are leaving the classroom, Nikumbh reveals to Ishaan that he too experienced the same difficulties with dyslexia. Nikumbh then visits the school's principal and obtains his permission to become Ishaan's tutor. He attempts to improve Ishaan's reading and writing by using remedial techniques developed by dyslexia specialists. Ishaan soon develops an interest in language and mathematics, and his grades improve.

Towards the end of the movie, in an art fair, there are two battles which happen – one within Ishaan to finally come out of the inner prison that he has been in for so long and one between the world and Ishaan, the kid who doesn't exist. In the end, Ishaan emerges victorious on both fronts, his talent triumphing over all odds and establishing his prowess in front of the entire world, but more importantly, in his own eyes. The film dealt with a critical issue of dyslexia and child education.

This movie shows parents sometimes without understanding kids punish them in a way that can destroy the child's whole personality. Albeit they want to do it for the betterment of the kid, they unknowingly harm their loved ones. Taare Zameen Par, like an elegant piece of poetry, beautifully presented emotions like happiness, fear and loneliness. The songs of Taare Zameen Par are like flowers in a bouquet, portraying everybody's emotions in a garland of expressive words and music.

Be it the sentimental and touching song 'Maa', which conveyed the insecurities of a child when sent away from home or the title song 'Taare Zameen Par' which took the audience to a world with unlimited possibilities. 'Jame Raho' was a situational and imaginative track, while 'Mera Jahan' gives a view of the child protagonist's naïve world.

The movie shows that how emotions of a child should be handled with lots of warmth, care, love, affection and, most importantly, with understanding so they can blossom.

Critical Acclaim of Taare Zameen Par

In the words of the film's director, Aamir Khan, "Taare Zameen Par is a film about children and it is a film which celebrates the abilities of children… The title has a very positive feel to it."

The movie received positive reviews all over. Subhash K. Jha suggests that the film is "a work of art, a water painting where the colours drip into our hearts, which could easily have fallen into the motions of over-sentimentality." Rajeev Masand of CNN-IBN argued that the true power of the film lies in its "remarkable, rooted, rock-solid script, which provides the landscape for such an emotionally engaging, heart-warming experience." Manish Gajjar from the BBC stated that the film "touches your heart and moves you deeply with its sterling performances. [It is] a film full of substance!"

Primary data findings for Taare Zameen Par

A movie like Taare Zameen Par was bound to create a positive feel in the society. The film's objective was such that people recognise how every child is special and how they should be treated as such.

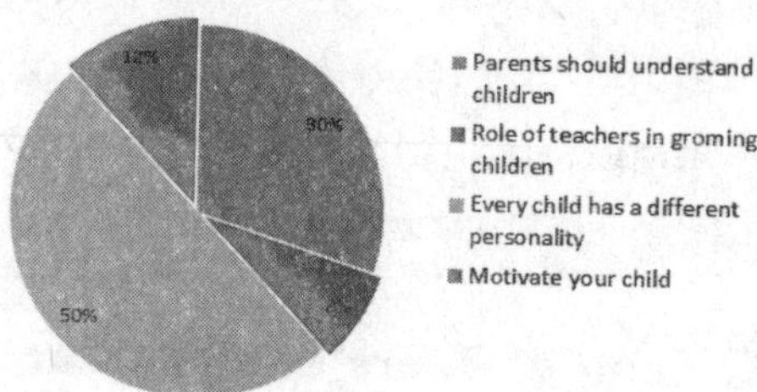

The top message comes out to be that cognizance of a different personality of every child. This is exactly what was intended from the movie, thus the subtitle "every child is special". There is also a suggestion that parents should try and understand their children better.

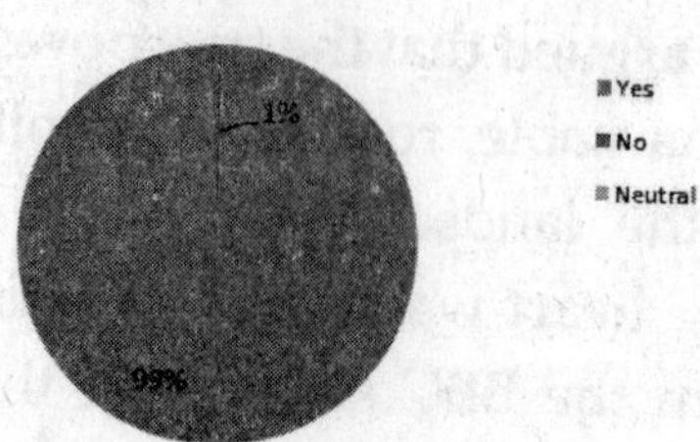

As is very apparent from the figure, almost the entire sample favourably responded to the question of Taare Zameen Par creating social awareness. This goes to show the kind of impact that a movie like Taare Zameen Par had.

Observations of Taare Zameen Par

Taare Zameen Par explores the life and imagination of a dyslexic eight-year-old child. The movie was an eye-opener for all parents who force their children to run in the rat race of daily life. In doing this, the parents tend to forget that each child has a special ability; Nikumbh becomes pied piper for the little, depressed and different Ishaan leading him to a blissful end.

Aamir Khan's Movies and Their Social Issues

These three movies just give a glimpse of how a Bollywood icon can impact the society through responsible choice of films. Although there are several other movies which also show contemporary social issues like Rang De Basanti, Peepli Live, etc., these three movies cater to a much wider audience in a more effective manner. Findings related to these three movies show that the society has gained a lot through these movies in terms of social awareness. Another important thing to note is the evolution of Aamir Khan as a youth icon.

Is Aamir Khan a youth icon through his work?

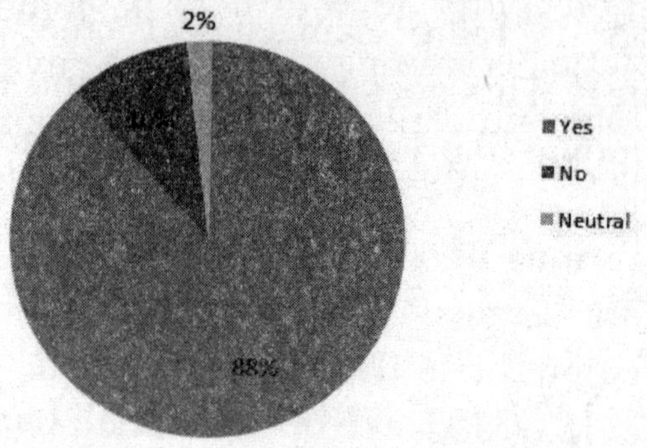

The findings clearly show that Aamir Khan is considered to be a youth icon, and that too by an overwhelming majority. Of course, it is not fully possible that his work alone brings a drastic change in the society, but his work has definitely sown seeds of social improvement. These issues are not just out there in the open. These issues are talked about in the drawing room of every house, on the corner of every street and in every function. Creating an impact here is a challenge and that is where the credit goes to Aamir Khan.

Aamir Khan used his stardom as a medium to give society in terms of creating awareness about social issues, which will be helpful in making society grow in positive direction. Although his journey was not pre-planned. As like a normal guy, he started his career to be a successful actor to achieve money, fame, stability, career but during this journey, he evolved himself as a social philanthropher who understands its responsibility to return back something to the society. Because people of India gave him so much of love and care. Very few people or, we can say, filmstars had used their image for the betterment of the society. Lagaan, 3 idiots, Tare Zameen Par. Our wish-list will be never-ending. We find his movies, specially when we are talking about these 3 movies, create a positive fuel in society. It has a great impact on the society, which shows in terms of Lagaan is added in management curriculum in IIM, Tare Zameen Par through which we came to know every child is special and how they should be treated in this technology age, emotions must be intact. 3 idiots gives the message that there will always be failures in the journey towards success, the important thing is to continue on that road. Another message for an individual, especially a student, should pursue something he/she is passionate about. The finding shows that Aamir Khan is considered to be a creater of awareness in society. Of course, it is not fully possible that his work alone brings a drastic change in the society, but at least he creates awareness towards it.

□

Courtesy : Aamir Khan @ Twitter

Courtesy : Google photos

Humse door jaoge kaise, dil se humen bhulaoge kaise ... hum wo khushboo hain jo saanson mein basti hai, khud ki saanson ko rok paoge kaise.

(FANAA)

6

Aamir Khan – The Family Man

His family calls him 'Captain Cautious'. A man always fuzzing overs family, ensuring that everyone is taken care of, worried about their well-being. He dotes on his children, niece and nephews and has tremendous respect for family elders.

Meet Aamir Khan's Family

Father: Late Tahir Hussain
Mother: Zeenat Hussain
Brother: Faisal Khan
Sister: Nikhat Khan
Sister: Farhat Khan
Wife: Kiran Rao
Ex-wife: Reena Dutta
Son: Junaid Khan
Daughter: Ira Khan
Son: Azad Rao Khan
Nephew: Imran Khan

Tahir Hussain – Father

Late Tahir Hussain, father of Aamir Khan, was

a film- maker, producer, director, screenwriter and actor. He also was the younger brother of well-known producer, director and writer Nasir Khan. He is related to Maulana Abul Kalam Azad.

He died on 2 February in the 2010 following a massive heart attack. He was just 71 at the time of his death. He had longed to live with Aamir's mother and his sons just before his death and therefore he moved to Bella Vista, Aamir's second flat in Bandra West. Just before he passed away, the family lived together.

Aamir was in US when his father died. He made all the security and other arrangements swiftly through phone. Security was handled by Ronit Roy who worked with Aamir since Lagaan days. By the time Aamir reached for the funeral, all arrangements were organised as per his instructions and he ensured a peaceful and dignified departure to his father.

Mr. Hussain, who divorced his first wife, Aamir's mother Zeenat in later years of his life and married Shanaaz who already had a son from a previous relationship, Hyder Ali Khan who was married (now separated) to TV actress Eva Grover. He produced films like *Madhosh* (1974), *Hum Hain Rahi Pyar Ke* (1993), *Tum Mere Ho* (1990), *Locket* (1986), *Dulha Bikta Hai* (1982), *Khoon Ki Pukaar* (1978), *Janam Janam Na Saath* (1977), *Zakhmee* (1975), *Anamika* (1973) and *Caravan* (1971).

Troubles brewed between Aamir Khan and his father regarding Aamir's brother Faisal's custody who went missing for around two days. He was then traced at a farmhouse near Khandala. Aamir said that his brother (Faisal) was suffering from schizophrenia whereas his dad claimed Faisal was suffering from a mild depression. Aamir wanted to keep his brother with himself as his dad was financially incapable to keep him. But his dad wanted to keep Faisal with him and Faisal too wanted to stay with his father at that point of time.

Aamir and his father both filed separate court applications seeking Faisal's custody. The court admitted both the applications and waited for medical report from J.J. hospital on Faisal's mental health. The medical report said that Faisal indeed suffers from schizophrenia as his brother Aamir had claimed. But Aamir lost the custody to his father as court decided to stick to Faisal's statement, who wanted to stay with his father. This was the only time when the actor (Aamir) went against his father which led to a tiff between them! Eventually, Tahir Khan realised Faisal needs special care and gave his custody to Aamir.

Zeenat Hussain – Mother

Aamir Khan's mother, Zeenat Hussain is a homemaker and the biggest influence in his life. As per his own admission, Aamir is quite like his mother-stubborn and determined. She was instrumental in making the firm base of character, strength and persistence in Aamir's life. She lives in the same complex as Aamir and they still are very close.

The 50-year-old actor kept his promise he made to his mother Zeenat Hussain by taking her to the holy land of Mecca. Even though he was busy working on forthcoming releases *Dhoom 3* and *Talaash,* he ensured that he fulfilled his mother's long-time wish. He launched the music of *Talaash* on October 19, shortly after returning from Chicago where he was shooting for *Dhoom 3* with co-stars Katrina Kaif and Abhishek Bachchan. He left for Mecca the same evening which clearly proves that Aamir's mother is his world.

Aamir spent quality time with his mother Zeenat in the holy city and helping her dutifully in fulfilling all the rituals. On October 22nd, the mother-son duo departed for Mina and performed Tawaf-e-Ziarat on October 26th. Then Aamir took his mother to Medina on October 29th and then boarded a flight back home.

Aamir adores his mother, "She is a wonderful person, and smashing to look at too!" he adds. His mother recalls fondly, "With his first pay cheque he bought me gold bangles and I was so taken aback."

Faisal Khan – Brother

Faisal Khan is the younger brother of Aamir Khan. His father launched him in movie *Madhosh* and Aamir acted with him in *Mela* in year 2000 which flopped.

Faisal played Shashi Kapoor's role as a child in the film *Pyaar Ka Mausam* in 1969. In 1988, he played a minor role as a villain in his brother Aamir's film *Qayamat Se Qayamat Tak*. He also played another small part in his brother's film *Jo Jeeta Wohi Sikandar* in the year 1992.

He was diagnosed Schizophrenia and accused Aamir with a lot of baseless accusation but Aamir maintained his dignity and stayed quiet.

There was a custody battle over him between Aamir and his father that garnered much press coverage. Faisal's custody was awarded to his father Tahir in 2007 as he did not wish to go with Aamir.

But after a week, Tahir submitted another application at the Metropolitan Magistrate's court saying that he wants to withdraw the custody application of Faisal. Tahir said that he has not been able to get in touch with his son for over 15 days (during the court's custody period of a month). After a month, Faisal was supposed to get a check-up done again at the J.J. Hospital to determine his mental health.

After Tahir filed the application, the press

finally started showing some restraint in reporting the developments as by then everybody had got the idea that Faisal needs to be taken care of. A lot of senior members of the press realised that Aamir was genuinely concerned about his brother.

However, Faisal again refused to go with his star brother and filed another application in the court saying that he wants to stay on his own. The court again granted him the permission and Faisal went to stay at a rented apartment at Tilak Nagar in Chembur.

Though the mainstream media by then had started to withdraw from reporting about Faisal, he continued to give out statements alleging that he is normal and his brother is trying to subdue him. But by then those statements had become less frequent.

About six months later, it was reported that Aamir was trying to reach out to his brother again. Faisal was living in Bandra East at that time and he too had realised that he needs Aamir back in his life.

Aamir and Faisal finally reconciled as the latter was spotted dropping onto the sets of *3 Idiots* to check on his brother often. They appeared to be cordial with each other. It was already 2009 and towards the end of that year, Faisal moved back to Bella Vista with Aamir.

Aamir made Faisal the Script Doctor at Aamir Khan Productions and he was responsible to screen the scripts sent to production house for consideration. He seemed satisfied with the role.

In better health now, he is ready to relaunch his career with a Kashmir-based love story, Chinar: A Destine of Love.

Nikhat Khan – Sister

Aamir Khan's elder sister Nikhat Khan is a part time film producer and painter. Nikhat helped produce her father's first directorial venture *Tum Mere Ho* in 1990 which featured her brother Aamir. She is married to Santosh Hegde and settled in Pune. Nikhat has two children Sehar and Shravan.

Nikhat celebrated her 50th birthday recently and Aamir Khan postponed his *Dhoom 3* shoot to celebrate his sister's birthday. On the very occasion, Nikhat was caught speaking about her family, Aamir Khan and her newly born nephew Azad Rao Khan. In a candid chit-chat, Nikhat revealed that Azad bears stark resemblance to Aamir Khan. She also added that Azad is cute and charming. He is picking up things like his daddy (Aamir). Aamir's mother, Zeenatji says that "there are certain distinct mannerisms which have an uncanny resemblance to Aamir". She not only spoke about Azad but also disclosed some interesting facts about Aamir Khan when he was a child. When asked whether Aamir used to pull her leg, she answered, "Not me, as I was the elder"!

The occasion also had actor Imran Khan present. Nikhat is the aunt of Imran. Imran being the first nephew, she shares a very good relationship with him!

She further adds, "It's not that we don't catch up now and then. But Aamir is so busy and always ends up getting calls in between when we meet".

Nikhat always keeps abreast of her bro's on screen life. She always watches his movies. Most of the time she watches it before the film releases to give her feedback or else she makes it a point to watch it on the very first day of the film's release. She never expected him to become an actor but she's glad he did!

Farhat Khan – Sister

Farhat Khan is the younger sister of Aamir Khan. She resides in the US along with her sons. Farhat is extremely close to her *bhaaijaan* and would often get bullied by him as a child as she was the youngest among the siblings!

Kiran Rao – Wife

Kiran Rao, wife of Aamir Khan, was born in Bangalore. She hails from a royal family (her grandfather J. Rameshwar Rao being the Raja of Wanaparthy). Kiran was raised in Kolkata where she received her education. She happens to be cousin to actress Aditi Rao Hydari.

She is currently a producer, screenwriter and director. Kiran started her career as an assistant director with Ashutosh Gowariker's *Lagaan*, where she met Aamir Khan. Aamir and Kiran ended up being together on the sets on *Lagaan*. The couple tied the knot on December 2005 after Aamir divorced his first wife Reena Dutta.

Aamir and Kiran currently reside in Bandra, Mumbai. They got blessed with a son via surrogacy on 5 December 2011 whom they named Azad Rao Khan (after Aamir's great-grand uncle, freedom fighter Maulana Abul Kalam Azad).

Reena Dutta – Ex-wife

Aamir Khan married his childhood sweetheart Reena Dutta on 18 April, 1986.

After 15 years of marriage, they filed for divorce by mutual consent in 2002. Even though the marriage ended, Reena is still close to the family and is seen at family functions of Khan household. Aamir says that Reena is an extremely important part of his family and will always be! Their relationship has undergone a change but he still has lots of love and respect for her in his heart. From legal point of view, they are divorced but the bond is not going to break with a piece of paper!

Junaid Khan – Son

Aamir Khan's elder son Junaid Khan was born

to his first wife Reena in Mumbai, Maharashtra. He is studying in South Mumbai College. Junaid is very passionate about his work like his father. He performed a street play along with his friends. Junaid organised and promoted cricket tournament for physically-challenged people.

Looks like Junaid is still figuring out what he wants to do. Once he makes up his mind and comes across a script that would suit him, Aamir will be more than happy to back him.

Junaid's sharp eye on film making – making impressed *3 Idiots* director Raj Kumar Hirani so much that he offered him opportunity to assist him in directing his next project *PK*, starring Aamir and actress Anushka Sharma in lead roles. The father-son duo shot for '*PK*' at Dilli Haat, a few days back.

Ira Khan – Daughter

Ira Khan is the second child of Aamir Khan and ex-wife Reena Dutta. Ira means watchful and that suits Ira's personality, she is a conscious and intelligent child. Aamir and Ira share a good father-daughter relationship. Currently, there are no reports about Ira's Bollywood debut but she did organise a charity celebrity football match in July 2015 to raise funds for an animal shelter for her aunt Nikhat's NGO.

Azad Rao Khan – Son

Aamir Khan and Kiran Rao became proud

parents of a baby boy on 1 December 2011. They named him Azad. Azad has been named after his great-grand uncle and great freedom fighter Maulana Abul Kalam Azad. Azad means free or liberated!

The baby was born through IVF to a surrogate mother at a private clinic in Bandra, Mumbai. Kiran got pregnant but unfortunately went through several miscarriages. Aamir Khan is proud to have a son through surrogacy. He already had two children, son Junaid and a daughter named Ira from his first wife Reena Dutta.

Imran Khan – Nephew

Aamir's nephew, Imran Khan was born on January 13, 1983. Imran started dating Avantika Malik since he was 19. The couple got engaged on 16 January 2010, in a farmhouse owned by Avantika's family in Karjat, near Navi Mumbai. They tied the knot a year later on 10 January 2011 in a private civil ceremony at Aamir Khan's home in Pali Hill. Imran and wife Avantika have a young daughter.

Imran Khan, who debuted in the silver screen industry with the movie *Jaane Tu Ya Jaane Naa,* has had a bad year at the box office with three of his releases; *Matru Ki Bijlee Ka Mandola, Once upon A Time in Mumbai Dobaara* and the recent Kareena Kapoor starrer *Gori Tere Pyaar Mein* failing to meet expectations.

Despite having a superstar *maamu* like Aamir Khan, the actor (Imran), who attempted to take risks and experiment with different roles, the movies eventually failed to impress at the box office. His current movie *Katti Batti* with Kangana Ranaut (Produced by Aamir Khan Productions) was not received well by audience due to a weak storyline.

□

Courtesy : Aamir Khan @ Twitter

Courtesy : Google photos

Duniya mein aaise-aaise heera paida hue hain, jinhone sari duniya ka naksha hi badal diya, kyun ki ye duniya ko apani alag nazar se dekh paaye.

(TAARE ZAMEEN PAR)

7
Aamir Khan The Marketing Genius

Marketing of QSQT

In 1998, in pre-social media marketing time, Aamir showed his talent of strategising film market through unconventional means. Aamir and his friend Raj Zutshi would go around Mumbai and post posters behind each auto rickshaw every evening after the movie's shooting was over. The poster had no photograph, just a tag line – Who is Aamir Khan? Ask the girl next door! This generated enough curiosity in the mind of Mumbaikars to know who this Aamir Khan was.

After the movie was released, everyone buying eight tickets or more was gifted with a poster of Aamir Khan.

Marketing for Ghajini

Aamir Khan gave Ghajini haircut to college students across the city. The ushers at cinema complex also adorned Ghajini haircut to bring familiarity with the lead character of the movie.

Marketing of 3 Idiots

During the promotional strategy for his film, *Talaash*, Aamir Khan shot a special episode, "Nayi Soch Ki Talaash Aamir Ke Saath", with the members of the Star Parivar at Film city, Goregaon.

Aamir Khan used various disguises and mingled around with people in different cities of the country for promotion of *3 Idiots*. He started the tour with city of his mother's birth, Benaras. He made friends with an auto rickshaw wala who helped him locate his mother's old house. He surprised his mother on phone with this info, as it was stated earlier.

He attended a wedding in Punjab, visited a school in Gujarat and gate crashed into Saurav Ganguly's house in Kolkata under disguise. He was totally himself with people and mingled around with people across the ages with such ease and humility which is endearing.

Marketing of PK

The first poster came out on 31 July 2014. A You Tube promotional video was also released on the same day. The second poster was launched on 20 August 2014 at an event in Mumbai. This poster was also released as a motion poster on YouTube. The new poster featured Aamir Khan wearing traditional Rajasthani attire, also sporting dark glasses and holding onto a brass tenor. The

Courtesy : Aamir Khan @ Twitter

promotional strategy for the movie was revealed by the makers at the launch of the second poster.

The third motion poster introduced Sanjay Dutt as Bhairon Singh with his trumpet. The fourth motion poster featuring Anushka Sharma along with Aamir Khan released on YouTube 16 October 2014. The poster introduced Anushka Sharma as Jagat Janani. Aamir Khan stated that *PK* will have a poster campaign in which a new poster would be introduced every two to three weeks. By the time of release, 8 to 10 posters would have been launched. The teaser released on 23 October 2014.

The film's first poster sparked a controversy as it featured Aamir posing almost nude with only an old radio cassette playing recorder covering his private parts. Although the Central Board of Film Certification had already cleared the film, a PIL was filed in the court by the All India Human Rights and Social Justice Front to ban its release saying it promoted nudity and vulgarity. The Supreme Court dismissed the plea and gave the film a green signal. A case was lodged against Aamir Khan and Rajkumar Hirani in Rajasthan.

□

Ab bhi jiska khoon na khaula, k
desh ke kaam na aaye, woh beka

8

Aamir Khan – Personal Facts Very Few Know (Quoting an Online/Print Interview of Aamir Khan)

Aamir Khan – Bollywood superstar, social activist, father of three and member of *Time* magazine's 100 most influential list – slips into the room, past two bodyguards and a small public relations army, with the air of an interloper. "Who me?" his cocked eyebrow seems to ask a roomful of international journalists at the Taj Land's End Hotel in Bandra, Mumbai. He is 49 but dressed like a teenager: in his board shorts, tight white superhero T-shirt and a blue baseball cap obscuring those famous baby-faced features and topaz eyes, he could be just another anonymous actor in this movie-obsessed town, home to the $2.2 billion Bollywood film industry.

But then he doffs his cap and emerges from camouflage, hiding in plain sight beneath his casual gear. There he is, one of the world's most famous actors, known to the bulk of India's 1.2 billion population as the star of countless Bollywood blockbusters during the past 25 years (including the industry's highest grossing film, international hit *Dhoom 3*), host of a nationally acclaimed, if controversial, talk show with an estimated audience reach of 600 million, magazine cover boy, and social justice crusader. He is courted by prime ministers and lauded by the likes of Oscar-winning *Slumdog Millionaire* composer A.R. Rahman, film director Shyam Bengal and actor Tom Hanks.

Namaste, Khan greets us cheerfully, steepling stocky hands and asking for chai.

In this room this morning, he's just a genial actor with a film to spruik. Outside, Khan is one of India's most powerful public figures, a Muslim megastar in a predominantly Hindu nation, Bollywood's first superstar activist, a man who has private meetings with Indian Prime Minister Narendra Modi, and who has lobbied for policy change on generic medicines, manual scavenging and female foeticide in India's Parliament and elsewhere. He has fended off numerous legal threats from angry targets of his TV show *Satyamev Jayate* ("no death threats yet, no"), and was mobbed by thousands of screaming fans last month as he toured New Delhi with British Prime Minister David Cameron. In a nation that worships its actors as deities, the cerebral actor is one of the brightest stars in the firmament.

We're here this morning to discuss Khan's latest movie, *PK*, to be released in Australia on December 19. Directed by Rajkumar Hirani, and produced by Vidhu Vinod Chopra (who early next year is releasing *Broken Horses*, India's first Hollywood film by a resident Indian director), it features Khan as a wide-eyed naif of mysterious origin. Press speculation has him playing an amnesiac or alien or God himself, but he ducks and weaves when pressed, saying little except it's 'dramedy' with a social message and that "it's probably one of the most challenging roles I've had in the last 25 years."

An astute marketer, Khan, more than anyone else in the business, it is said, understands the power of stoking demand through starving the press and public.

His formidable charm acts like a smokescreen: in melodious Hinglish, he soon has a roomful of frustrated journalists cracking up as he unspools, instead, a gossipy stream of comical impersonations (he does a mean Bhojpuri accent) of fellow actors and temperamental directors. He waxes lyrical about everything from his 'handloomer' theory of filmmaking, his reading list (John Kennedy Toole's *A Confederacy of Dunces*, Chitra Banerjee Divakaruni's *The Palace of Illusions*, Irvin Yalom's *When Nietzsche Wept*: Indians expect a certain intellectual heft from their film stars), to his awkwardness with tweeting and social media ("but no one is allowed to write for me").

He says he has loosened up and become less judgmental with age, and speaks of the "positive energy" his second wife, director Kiran Rao, has brought into his life. He addresses everything from why India seems to spawn so many film and political dynasties (PM Modi is not from a dynasty, he quickly points out), the perils for Muslim actors speaking out in a Hindu nation, and journalistic ethics (don't get in bed with your film sources, he earnestly advises), to the challenges facing Bollywood, from piracy to the influx of Hollywood films, and the history of sync sound in Indian filmmaking (there's a bit of a joyful film nerd there).

In a way, the mysterious *PK* symbolises Khan himself – elusive and shape shifting at his core, a maverick who has successfully plotted his own unorthodox path through Indian film. Born in Mumbai on March 14, 1965, to a middle-class Muslim film family (his father was producer Tahir Hussain, his uncle was filmmaker Nasir Hussain, his cousin is filmmaker Mansoor Khan, and his nephew is rising film star Imran Khan), Khan made his debut aged eight in Nasir Hussain's *Yaadon Ki Baaraat* in 1973. His breakthrough film came in Mansoor Khan's cult romantic blockbuster *Qayamat Se Qayamat Tak* (1988), and throughout the

1990s he dominated Hindi commercial cinema as one of three conquering Khans – the other two are Shah Rukh Khan and Salman Khan. (Interestingly, the three most powerful Bollywood actors are all Muslim.) Critically-acclaimed roles in *Raakh, Raja Hindustani, Rang De Basanti* and *Fanaa* followed; in 2001, he made his debut as a producer in the Academy Award-nominated *Lagaan,* where he played the leader of a ragtag bunch of villagers battling the British over an unfair tax. Then came 2008's thriller *Ghajini,* and monster international hits *3 Idiots* and *Dhoom 3.*

Khan also has a huge international following across the vast Indian diaspora, from the US and Britain to Dubai, Singapore and Australia, which is now the fifth biggest overseas market for Indian cinema. Mitu Bhowmick Lange, head of Mind Blowing Films which distributes Indian films here in partnership with Hoyts, says Khan's films are highly popular in Australia, with *Dhoom 3* taking out the top award for highest grossing foreign film in Australia (it took $1.72 million) at the Australian International Movie Convention on the Gold Coast last year. "Only two Indian films have crossed the $1 million mark in Australia, *3 Idiots* and *Dhoom 3,* and both star Aamir Khan. He is not just a movie star, he is a cultural icon," she says.

Asked about his huge following in Australia and elsewhere, Khan says: "I personally believe if a film is well-made and good, it travels. Cinema is not restricted by language or physical boundaries."

The actor could easily have kept on a lucrative path of romantic and action blockbusters but opted for a different trajectory, making only one or two films a year (unusual in an industry where leading actors can churn out more than eight a year), and building an eclectic repertoire of roles – amnesiac avenger, reclusive artist, nationalist rebel, apathetic college kid, special education teacher – across an unusually varied slate of films, many with a social justice bent, tackling everything from political corruption to caste to Indian's troubled higher education system.

His credits range from Deepa Mehta's arthouse film *Earth* to the unexpected hit *Taare Zameen Par*, where he played an art teacher captivated by a dyslexic student. Of his limited annual output, Khan says he can't concentrate on more than one film at a time ("it's like a traditional handloomer; once they put the thread on, they can't put anything else on until they've finished making the sari or whatever"), and says he chooses films on their emotional pull and "not on commerce." There's a shrewd pragmatic streak behind the idealism, however; he is a sharp reader of audience moods and tastes, and will often subsidise his more niche films because while "I will make whatever I want, I will make sure no one – exhibitors, producers, distributors – loses money."

He has had his flops, certainly, but his off-beat choices have often struck gold; influential film critic Anupama Chopra says: "Aamir has the instinct for a great story." In an industry dominated by box-office figures, Khan prizes the organic, laborious process of filmmaking rather than the end result. He says bluntly that "you can safely assume 90 per cent of the production houses giving out figures are not giving accurate figures so you should take it with a sackful of salt. Don't believe that records are being broken every three months."

Also unorthodox is his laissez-faire approach to fame and his public image. In an industry where flamboyant self-promotion reigns, Khan rarely attends film award ceremonies – he also audaciously declined Madame Tussauds' offer of a wax statue in London – and keeps a relatively low profile. Unlike fierce rival Shah Rukh Khan, whom Forbes India branded 'Shah Rukh Inc.' courtesy of a vast commercial empire worth more than $US600 million ($ 700m), Aamir Khan does not heavily invest in brand-building. "I think that should be something that happens organically," he says.

If Shah Rukh Khan is Mr Corporate, and the musclebound, trouble-prone Salman Khan is the nation's lovable jock, then Aamir Khan is Bollywood's thinker and intellectual. A report in *India Today,* crunching box-office averages for their last seven films, neatly delineates the differences thus: "Salman is the Khan of the Indian Box Office, Aamir is the Khan of Quality, and Shah Rukh is the Khan of Wealth." The report also revealed the net worth of Aamir Khan, incidentally, was $ 180m, compared with Salman Khan at $ 200m and SRK at $ 600m.

Asked about the curious phenomenon of Muslim dominance in Indian film, he says while there has always been a strong Islamic presence in Bollywood, from actors Dilip Kumar and Feroz Khan to directors such as Naseeruddin Shah, it's mere coincidence. "We are almost the same age, born in 1965 or thereabouts, all three of us became popular in our own ways and remained popular for 25 years, which in itself is unusual. What it does indicate, however, is that it speaks well of the people of India, the fact that the majority is of a particular religion and the three stars that the country loves happens to be of a different religion."

Khan is arguably singular in Bollywood for his social justice activism, exemplified in his TV show, *Satyamev Jayate* ("Truth Alone Prevails"). Launched in May 2012, its opening episode tackled the scourge of female foeticide that has left some Indian states with dangerously lopsided sex ratios ("The whole of Mother India has bathed in the blood of her daughters," Khan emotionally told his viewers). Across the three highly rating seasons to date, it has attracted an audience of almost 600 million in India who tune in for weekly episodes, blending hard-hitting journalism with tabloid-style storytelling (it has been dubbed "part *Oprah*, part *60 Minutes*") tackling everything from domestic violence, the killing of brides in dowry disputes, alcoholism, mental health, caste inequities, medical malpractice and child sex abuse.

The show has taken the deeply conservative nation by storm: since its debut, more than 13 million people have posted on the show's website; an episode on alcohol abuse sparked an unprecedented 60,000 phone calls flooding the Alcoholics Anonymous helpline. After Khan broadcast a sting operation filming more than 100 doctors offering to illegally abort female foetuses, authorities in Rajasthan – with one of the nation's worst gender ratios – ordered an investigation into doctors and clinics believed to be conducting such illegal procedures.

Khan, capitalising on his enormous audience reach to push for policy change, has addressed the Indian Parliament on the need for price control and cheaper drugs, and attracted the wrath of Indian doctor groups and the pesticide lobby following episodes on medical malpractice and toxic farming. "There is a large majority of people who see the show and love it, these are people who want change and who are not happy with the way things are. And there is a very, very minuscule percentage of people who are actually happy with the status quo and don't want change. They're the ones who get upset."

His work has caught the eye of the international press, with an Asian edition of *Time* in 2012 featuring him on the cover as "India's first superstar-activist ...can one actor change a nation?", followed by his inclusion last year in *Time*'s 100 Most Influential list (he was one of only seven featured on separate covers, joining the likes of schoolgirl advocate Nobel Laureate Malala). In a glowing profile, A.R. Rahman said his show bravely "confronts India's deepest social ills, from sexual abuse to caste discrimination. He uses his gifts as a charmer to give his audience the most bitter medicine." Actor Hanks has said: "Few celebrities take the initiative of coming forward to change the society and he has done a remarkable job."

It's not all praise, of course: critics have accused him of everything from being overly emotional and cashing in on social misery to offering simplistic solutions to complex problems, and doing it for cynical self-promotional reasons. Asked about the criticism, Khan is steely: unconstructive criticism "is like water off a duck's back." He also dismisses speculation that he is using the show as a platform for a leap into politics: he believes artists have a wider responsibility "to try to strengthen the social fabric of society" through art and believes he can be more effective as an actor working "from the bottom up rather than top down sitting in Parliament."

More than most, he understands the power of TV and film in a nation with high pockets of illiteracy. As to why so few of his Bollywood peers have done the same, he is defensive, citing the work of film legend Amitabh Bachchan as the face of a polio campaign. He reveals that he was advised by many not to take on the show in case it damaged his popularity: "Whether it has affected my career I don't know, but as a human being, I feel certainly closer to the realities of my country and what people go through."

Talk turns to the challenges facing Bollywood, which celebrated its 100th anniversary last year and is regarded as the biggest movie ticket market in the world with an output annually of 1200 films. It has undergone vast changes, transformed by India's own seismic cultural shifts as well as the influx of foreign investment via giants such as 20th Century Fox and Walt Disney, which has seen the rise of sophisticated international distribution networks and multiplexes catering to the burgeoning middle class. Khan welcomes the broadening of the cheesy song-and-dance template that once dominated the industry (he is scathing about the "disco era" of the 1970s and 80s film-making scene) and the industry's embrace of contemporary themes that explore everything from artificial insemination to urban gang warfare and premarital sex.

But he's aware of key challenges, including that of piracy (a leading director, Anurag Basu, has said it costs the industry about $US3.34 billion and 60,000 jobs every year). Khan thinks "it can be tackled, if not fully eradicated, if – and it's a big if – the industry works together." He suggests a solution that he sees as a "game changer": building more theatres across the nation and offering tickets at far cheaper prices – 25 rupees as compared to 300 rupees – for the poorer masses who don't go to the cinema.

The biggest problem he sees is the failure of the industry to capitalise on India's size: "Our population is 1.2 billion but the theatre-going audience for our biggest hits is around three to four crore (30 to 40 million). That's not even 5 per cent."

India is one of the few markets where its own product dominates the box office, but there are questions raised by the growing impact of Hollywood films, although it represents only 9 per cent of box office. Khan is unperturbed. He believes Indian audiences will always remain loyal to their indigenous filmmaking because of a certain "emotional key" and connection to their local fare: they will always be fundamentally more attached to "a Shah Rukh, or an Aamir, or Salman, much more than, say, Hugh Jackman." Khan's PR flak is making frantic wind-up motions after a marathon session, and the actor, finally, rises to his feet.

"All good?" he asks, then smiles to a chorus of cheers. He praises the "good energy" of the session, poses obligingly for photos in front of a giant promotional poster, and with that he's gone, baseball cap crammed low, in hiding once again from the ever-present waiting throngs outside.

We know that Aamir Khan's flawless acting is loved by one and all. However, Aamir has got an ardent fan offshore as well. This fan is a renowned British film critic – Peter Bradshaw. When *Lagaan* released in 2001, Peter had showered a lot of praises on the film. He had said, "Larger than life and outrageously enjoyable, it's got a dash of spaghetti western, a hint of Kurosawa, with a bracing shot of Kipling. Ashutosh Gowariker's film is virile, muscular storytelling, with rich musical dance numbers. A heavily bewhiskered Chris England plays a vicious bodyline bowler. Go and see it."

Years later, Peter is on his India visit and has not forgotten Aamir. He expressed his desire to meet the perfectionist star. He said, "They're mammoth names and I would be delighted to meet them. Aamir is the Titanic of Bollywood and I understand how packed his schedule is. If he has the time, I'm looking forward to a chat."

Peter will attend the two-day workshop at the

MAMI Young Critics Lab in Mumbai. He said, "I'm going to emphasise on commitment, engagement and passion. Hollywood has long given up on the musical genre and this is why Bollywood is so vital."

The Rise of the Star

In Aamir, one sees a curiosity which spurs him on to earn all the time. If anything interests him, he delves into it so minutely that after figuring out himself he is able to explain it to others equally clearly.

Aamir had a very clear perception of what was true for him, he may not have always been right but that did not stop him from being clear about his priorities. If he was wrong, he was well prepared to accept it. Yet he never dithered in taking decisions for fear of being wrong. All his decisions have been taken by him with great clarity and responsibility.

Ironically, the industry 'accuses' Aamir of professionalism, a quality which is usually seen as a virtue, is in him seen as a vice. He justified this, "See I'm very professional as far as my responsibilities go and in what is expected of me but I'm not professional when it gets down to achieving what is required to be achieved. Suppose I am expected to work eight hours a day but the shoot is not over and the eight hours are up and we still have to achieve the shot or scene. I will extend those eight hours to twelve or sixteen or whatever is required to finish what we set out to do. If I was strictly professional I'd say, sorry my eight hours are over I have to go, or sorry I'm just an actor why should come and select which banner or website to put my film under? Once I'm doing a film I see it as my film and if the producer or director or anybody from the unit calls upon me to see what they're doing I'd love to do that. It doesn't bother me that it's eating into my time to do so. I think I'm an emotional person, I work emotionally, I give. But what is required of me professionally, from that point of view I'm very professional. And. I would do this for every film because I enjoy working that way. I enjoy achieving the best possible result for whatever we are doing, whether we're making a film or doing an interview or playing a game of chess. I want to enjoy doing it to the fullest, so I don't want to compromise at that time."

This is merely the beginning of another journey for this actor/producer who enjoys his stardom but does not operate from it. One can but say that fourteen years is a long time to receive his due but he has waited patiently for it. He reiterates, "I want to be the best loved star in the country!"

As an actor, when he made his debut in *Qayamat Se Qayamat Tak,* Aamir Khan was seen as the typical chocolate faced hero with limited potential. He was too cute, too short, too small built to be anything but a romantic hero. What the public did not see was this newcomer's ambition and resilience. He was a survivor and he has worked hard at living down the first assessment made of him.

Own focus found its mark with directors like Dharmesh Darshan [*Raja Hindustani*], Mathew Mathan [*Sarfarosh*] and even newcomers like Vikram Bhatt [*Ghulam*] and Ram Varma [*Rangeela*]. All these films were such massive hits that Aamir got himself the reputation of the star whose films were sure to succeed. He seemed to have found a formula for success; something no one has been able to do. Every newcomer director wanted Aamir in his film to ensure that it was a success. This meant he now had to deliver on the expectations he had raised. Strangely enough, he had driven himself into a corner where nothing but success would succeed. It was as if the actor was saying – "Expect nothing but the best from me." Ironically as an Aamir watcher, I've always wished that the actor had a larger, more varied repertoire of expressions – he seems to be limited, inhibited almost, by something one cannot quite put a finger to, but he struggles hard to get past it. One often feels he does not let go enough, as if some inner driver holds the reins too tightly for him to break free. Ironically, his actions are all appropriate to the character he is portraying but his expression often isn't. Dil Chahta Hai asked more of him in the letting go department and to do him justice he tried his best but it still was not enough. This makes one realise that Aamir will still grow as an actor, still extract something from within to reach a height which perhaps he himself has not envisaged as yet.

Though his film *Lagaan* succeeded magnificently, it was perhaps *Dil Chahta Hai* that showcased a different side of the star. Which proves that Aamir works beautifully in tandem with a director who is clear about what he requries.

The honest, unbending police officer of *Sarfarosh*; the care couldn't less but nevertheless sensitive *tapori* of *Rangeela*; the honest to goodness taxi driver of Raja Hindustani; the careless romeo of *Dil Chahta Hai* and of course the committed Bhuvan of *Lagaan*.

□

Courtesy : Aamir Khan @ Twitter

> Sunny Leone@SunnyLeone Sep 21
> Hey @aamir_khan saw you in the Snapdeal Ad. Motte or not, you still look hot! Love you. https://youtu.be/yCiM_JyA1Nw;)
> 496 retweets 950 favorites
> Aamir Khan @aamir_khan Sep 24
> Thank you @SunnyLeone, you are too kind. Love. a.
> RETWEETS 1,403 FAVORITES 2,945
> 7:42 AM – 24 Sep 2015. Details

In early 2016, Sunny Leone was subjected to an embarrassing interview by a misogynist TV reporter where he said Sunny would never get to work with actors like Aamir Khan due to her past. The interview drew much flake and also a response from Aamir Khan saying he would like to work with Sunny whenever there is an opportunity.

Later, Aamir shared a meal with Sunny and her husband Daniel Weber in Delhi while they were in the capital for their respective assignments.

Flashback

You may recall the 1992 advt. of Lehar Pepsi with Aamir Khan, Mahima Chaudhary and Sanju (Aishwarya Rai). The advertisement was an instant hit amongst the youth.

Aamir Khan's journey as a brand ambassador had started after release of his initial movies such as *Qayamat Se Qayamat Tak*. He endorsed motorbike HERO PUCH and was visible in their advertisement.

Courtesy : Aamir Khan @ Twitter

Courtesy : Google photos

Perfection ko improve karna mushkil hota hai.

(DIL CHAHTA HAI)

9

Aamir Khan– The Brand Ambassador

Over the years, Aamir has endorsed many leading brands and has effectively turned around their fortunes or reposition their market standing. Here is snippet of some of the brands he endorsed.

Brand Ambassador of Snapdeal

The latest brand Aamir Khan had been endorsing is Snap deal, the online e-commerce site. The advertisement showed the actor promoting various aspects of sandal, making it the preferred site for online shopping (connecting with manufacturers, ease of delivery, discounts, etc.) Such is his fan following, actress Sunny Leone posted the following tweet on the micro blogging site Twitter, where Aamir has 14.7 million followers (and growing) and Aamir's humble response to the praise bestowed upon him.

Sunny Leone@SunnyLeone Sep 21 Hey @aamir_khan saw you in the Snapdeal Ad. Motte or not, you still look hot! Love you. https://youtu.be/yCiM_JyA1Nw;) 496 retweets 950 favorites Aamir Khan @aamir_khan Sep 24 Thank you @SunnyLeone, you are too kind. Love. a. RETWEETS 1,403 FAVORITES 2,945 7:42 AM – 24 Sep 2015. Details

In early 2016, Sunny Leone was subjected to an embarrassing interview by a misogynist TV reporter where he said Sunny would never get to work with actors like Aamir Khan due to her past. The interview drew much flake and also a response from Aamir Khan saying he would like to work with Sunny whenever there is an opportunity.

Later, Aamir shared a meal with Sunny and her husband Daniel Weber in Delhi while they were in the capital for their respective assignments.

Flashback

You may recall the 1992 advt. of Lehar Pepsi with Aamir Khan, Mahima Chaudhary and Sanju (Aishwarya Rai). The advertisement was an instant hit amongst the youth.

Aamir Khan's journey as a brand ambassador had started after release of his initial movies such as *Qayamat Se Qayamat Tak*. He endorsed motorbike HERO PUCH and was visible in their advertisement.

BRAND AMBASSADOR

COKE

Aamir was brand ambassador of Coke (Cocacola) for almost a decade and showed his acting prowess in different get ups and catchy advt. over the years. To capture audience's imagination in span of one to one and a half minute is an art, Aamir was learnt very well. Each of his Coke advt, be as a Punjabi Jatt pulling out coke chilled in a well through pulley to impress city girls or a Bihari babu impressing village belle by saving them from cheating while promoting *'Thanda Matlab panach'* or the Bengali Babu sipping down all bottles of coke under pretext of doubting the quality of the product or the Chinese man asking for samosa and thanda saying *'madhumakkhi kaat gayi thi, main chinese nahi hoon'*. Each Advt left a recall value in millions of hearts.

As a Nepali Sherpa, as a waiter in train, as a taper in hotel, as double role of himself, he used different get ups and style to put cross the message deep into the television watcher's mind *'thunda matlab cocacola'*.

TITAN

Aamir's sauve representation of a sentimental man with connect to his Titan watch collection and connecting it to life events such as an advt with Zohra Sehgal playing his dadi and gifting her a watch if she does not find a groom for herself. Aamir's presence helped the brand to regain their position to imported watched endorsed by other celebrities. He was able to put across the message of 'Be More' to the audience.

Also the jargon, *'kaam bada ya chota nahi hota, kaam kaam hota hai'*.

He played a charmer in advt with Jacqueline Fernandes in promo advt of Titan Purple.

TATA SKY and TATA SKY PLUS

He was convincing as a pesty sales man in retail showroom or overbearing haircutter Ram Milan at a saloon or the greedy milkman or a distraught sardaar ji in the Tata Sky advt. conveying the jargon *'Isko Laga dala to life jhingalala'*.

As a typical young husband in an urban household in Tata Sky Plus advt., he played the role lovingly and in most convincing way. Be it talking to mother-in-law or recording cricket match or going out for dinner and record favourite movie, he used tease and humour to put across his message.

TOYOTA INNOVA

Aamir played multiple characters travelling together in a car to highlight salient features of the SUV.

GODREJ

SAMSUNG MOBILE (Year 2008)

MAHINDRA STALLIO

PARLE G BUISCUIT

□

10

Trivia on Aamir Khan

1. Who among Bollywood stars can create a serial such as Satyamev Jayate based on pertinent issues burning our social sphere. Stand for the girl child or support much controversial Article 377 and provide a platform for LGBT activists to voice their concerns?
2. He has shared dias with social activists like Medha Patkar and Anna Hazare, supporting their causes, even at the cost of his own movie's well-being (cąse in point Fanaa was banned in Gujarat due to his support on Narmada bate Andolan).
3. His movies and serials was based on pertinent issues.

   2006 Rang De Basanti

   2007 Taare Zameen Par

   2009 3 Idiots

   2011 Peepli Live

   2012 Satyamev Jayate

   2014 PK

4. *Lagaan* was only Bollywood movie of last decade which came close to shortlisted in final five in Best Foreign Film category in Oscar. Aamir Khan has seven Filmfare awards, four National Awards, Padma Sri from Indian Government in the year 2003 and Padma Bhushan in the year 2010.
5. Besides, did you know that he was awarded the **Padma Shree** in 2003 and the **Padma Bhushan** India's third highest Civil Honour in 2010 by the Government of India.
6. He is the **brand ambassador** of the government–organised IEC campaign to raise **awareness about malnutrition.**
7. He is the **UNICEF** goodwill brand ambassador for India.
8. He featured on the cover of *Time* Magazine-August 2012.
9. Finally, the mood of Bollywood is changing. We are looking at a generation of directors who are interested in making quality non-masala movies. Those guys have an audience partially because of this guy. He changed the trend and made subject-based movies. *Dhobi Ghat* was one such movie.

Microsoft Chairman Bill Gates had expressed an interest to meet with Aamir Khan in year 2013 and discuss with him the social issues faced by India. This wish came true recently when he joined

Aamir Khan and Prannoy Roy in an interactive chat session in New Delhi.

Bill Gates, through his NGO 'Bill and Melinda Gates Foundation' is conducting research on diseases prevalent in many countries including India and inventing new vaccines for these. He mentions in his blog that he tries to visit India every year to follow up on these developments. This time, he met up with Aamir Khan and in the chat session, discussed India's long journey to better health.

In the past, bollywood actors shied away from adapting to their characters in movies. Shahrukh Khan remained Shahrukh Khan whether he was a lover or a villain. Amitabh Bachchan's Vijay was repeated throughout his career. It was Aamir who broke this trend by portraying realistic characters and delivering successful films.

He portrayed diverse roles and was able to get under the skin of his characters. He changed his style, lingo and even body language to convey the characters realistically, from a villager of 18th century in Lagaan to a Delhi-boy in *Rang De Basanti.*

Aamir Khan is a superstar, his opportunities, choices, risks, expectations and fan following must be most similar to other superstars rather than say a newcomer, a character actor and therefore by relative comparison between those who are considered by media and people as equals only can rating be done.

His plus points are:

1. Commitment to a character: Many critics have said that his portrayal is rarely loose and his body language, facial expressions, delivery and emotions are mostly in tune with the character. Compare that to Shah Rukh Khan whose body language and style in almost every movie is that of a teenage romancer and Salman Khan and Akshay Kumar who have hard time understanding where they end and their character begins and you will see that Aamir Khan is way ahead.

2. Commitment to a project: One movie, one year (atleast). From which other superstar can you expect this?

3. Movies of matter: *Rang De Basanti, 3 Idiots, Lagaan, Taare Zameen Par, Dhobi Ghat.* Sure he does some commercial movies, but he's still better than those who make movies just for the sake of crossing the 100 crore revenue mark.

4. Movies that matter: *Rang De Basanti*, at the very least, was partly responsible for bringing the concept of peaceful protest and non-violent agitations in vogue. Due to the massive uproar, Jessica Lall murder which had been closed got so much media attention that the judiciary had to review it and deliver speedy justice. *Taare Zameen Par* brought to the fore the needs of patients of dyslexia.

Lagaan is the closest thing Bollywood came to an Oscar in the past decade or so.

The only seven Indian Movies that are in the IMDb top 250

Taare Zameen Par

3 idiots

Rang De Basanti

Dil chahta hai

Gangs of Wasseypur

Lagaan

Shades

Out of seven, five are Aamir Khan starrers. That proves the mettle of the actor with towering personality, Aamir Khan.

□

Courtesy : Aamir Khan @ Twitter

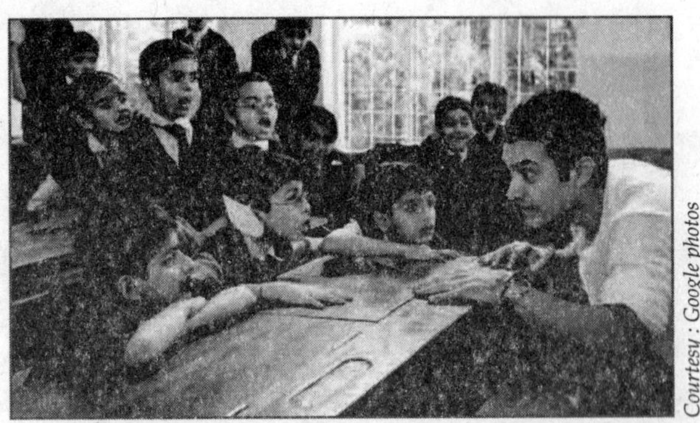

Courtesy : Google photos

Khayal karna bahut zaroori hai, is mein ilaaj ki shakti hai, ek marham hai jismein dard milta hai.

(TAARE ZAMEEN PE)

11

Aamir's in His Own Words (Year 2012)

Aamir Khan's Column in the Hindu

Let's give marriage the importance it deserves in every sense, financial, emotional, mental.

—Aamir Khan

Marriage is a terribly important part of life. It's a partnership you form, a companion you choose, hopefully for the rest of your life. Someone who helps you, who supports you and vice versa. The way we view marriage and the way we approach it determines how our life could end up being.

Today, I want to largely address youngsters, because most of you who are older are already married and for better or worse have already made your choices.

In India, we spend so much of our emotions, thoughts, time and money (that which we have, and that which we borrow), towards marriage. But do we actually spend all this time, effort, money and emotion towards marriage? I think not. In fact, we concentrate all of these resources not on our marriage, but on our wedding day.

'*Bade dhoom dhaam se shaadi*', is probably one of the most common phrases in India. There's so much of emotion, thought, focus, all concentrated on the 'event': "How will I look on that one day?" "How will society perceive me and my chosen partner?" "What will they say about the wedding arrangements?" "What will they say about the invitation card?" "What will they say about the food?" "What will they say about the clothes?"

Now, this 'they' we refer to are our friends, our relatives and other people in society whom we are acquainted with, and whom we hope to invite. And most of our energy goes towards making this one day a success. Often, even our choice of spouse is in some way linked with the driving need to make the day perfect. Haven't all of us heard these statements: "*Meri beti* engineer *se shaadi karegi.*" "*Meri beti* IAS *se shaadi kar rahi hai.*" "My daughter is marrying an NRI." We imagine that people admire such choices, and their admiration makes us happy. We allow our choice of spouse to very often be dictated by how people will perceive us. But the hard truth is that 'they' are not going to spend the rest of their life with the groom or the bride.

Sometimes we simply choose the *'khandaan,'* the family or the aura surrounding the family, and not the individual himself or herself. "My son is marrying so and so's daughter." "My daughter is marrying such and such's son." We tend to focus, not on the groom or bride but on the label attached to him or her.

Now let's examine a few other important aspects of marriage.

Time

After we've spent the bulk of our time worrying about others' perceptions, we spend tons of time deciding what to wear. We do intense R&D on honeymoon destinations. We spend time discussing arrangements, menus, guest lists. All of these are great cause for arguments. All this time is being spent in preparation for 'the day.' But how much time do we spend on the most critical decision – selecting the correct life partner? Who is the girl I'm marrying? Who is the boy I'm planning to spend the rest of my life with? Don't we want to know them as human beings? Understand his or her nature, value system? Are we on the same wavelength? Is there compatibility? Does he or she have a sense of humour? Is this the person with whom I want to spend the rest of my life? Instead of taking ample time to make this very crucial decision, very often, marriages are fixed after just one meeting. "*Chalo baat pakki hogayi. Muh meetha karo.*"

In India, most marriages are arranged. We check on the prospective groom's/bride's family, caste, home, education, income, bank balance, appearance and complexion. But all of these things are purely superficial. Why don't we utilise the same time and effort in understanding the human being we are about to (hopefully) spend the rest of our life with?

Should you agree to spend the rest of your life with someone just because he/she carries an attractive label such as IIT or MBBS? Is one marrying the person or the label? Shared interests, like-mindedness, companionship, shared sensibility, sense of humour – shouldn't all this matter?

Money

We spend a lot of money on the wedding day. The rich spend beyond measure – each competing with the other in extravagance. The middle class or working class pours all its earnings and savings into the wedding. If you have the money, by all means decide how you want to spend it. But for those who are not wealthy, for whom every rupee earned is precious, for whom a daughter's wedding means pouring everything you have earned, or saved, it means breaking fixed deposits, selling assets and taking loans. Instead of spending all that money on the wedding day, why not decide to take the amount set aside for the girl's wedding and give it to her to use to kick-start her new life with her spouse? Instead of that lavish function, why not just have a simple, *sharbat* wedding and give the girl the money instead? It will be so useful for her life? I believe *sharbat* weddings are a great idea. Call as many people as you desire, serve them a soft drink and say thank you for coming and for blessing the newlyweds.

Have fun. Enjoy the day. Make merry. But with simplicity.

Youngsters, tell your parents, "We don't want a big function. Let me use the money for something important that helps my life. Let me use the money to invest in building the foundation for a happy married life."

Emotions

All our emotions are trained on 'that day.' What will happen on that day? What will people think and say? How happy will I be that day? Will the day be memorable? But instead, should we not be thinking of how we will feel for the next 40 years of married life? Let's not barter one day of happiness for a lifetime of unhappiness. Our emotions need to be invested not in that one day, but in a lifetime.

Think about life ahead, not just that one day. Let's give marriage the importance it deserves –

in every sense, financial, emotional, mental. Let's give it our time, emotions and energies to plan those years that lie ahead. Therefore, the key is the person you have chosen as your life partner. That is the only element you should be thinking of and no other. And please take your time over that decision. Understand, probe, check, go deep. The better you do this, the happier life is likely to be. Take the step of marrying only when you are fully satisfied about the character and temperament of the person you are marrying.

Dowry I am totally opposed to. This is a retrograde practice, and also illegal. Think about it – can a relationship, built on the foundation of money and greed, ever be meaningful or beautiful? Should we not invest in our daughter's education instead of saving up for her dowry? Make her so accomplished and independent that she is capable of crafting her own future, and becomes the master of her own happiness. Then she won't need a greedy, useless groom to complete her life. Let her marry a person who respects her. Let her marry a man who she believes is worthy of her. Whom she is happy to spend the rest of her life with.

Satyamev Jayate!

□

Courtesy : Aamir Khan @ Twitter

Courtesy : Google photos

Kahane ko to ek round sirf do minute ka hota hai ... par socha jaaye to do minute mein 120 second hote hain ... us ek second ka intezaar kar jab samne wala galati kare.

(DANGAL)

12

Aamir Khan – The King of Box Office

In top 10 highest grossing Indian movies of all times, four of the movies have Aamir Khan in the lead cast, with his latest movie DANGAL at the top with a worldwide gross collection of US $110 million. This speaks volumes about his global popularity and mass following.

Global Gross Box Office Collections figures

Movie	Year	Studio(s)/ Producers	Language	Worldwide	Gross
DANGAL	2016	WALT DISNEY PICTURES AAMIR KHAN PRODUCTIONS UTV MOTION PICTURES	HINDI	₹ 730 Crores	(US$110 MILLION)
PK	2014	VIDHU CHOPRA FILMS	HINDI	₹ 735 CRORES	(US$110 MILLION)
DHOOM 3	2013	YASHRAJ FILMS	HINDI	₹ 536 CRORES	(US$81 MILLION)
3 IDIOTS	2009	VIDHU CHOPRA FILMS	HINDI	₹ 392 CRORES	(US$59 MILLION)

Highest Grossing Hindi Films

The Hindi film industry, based in Mumbai India, is frequently known as Bollywood. Bollywood is one of the largest film producers in India and one of the largest centres of film production in the world.

In top 10 highest grossing Hindi movies of all times, four of the movies have Aamir Khan in the lead cast, with his latest movie DANGAL at the top with a Worldwide Gross collection of US $110 million.

□

Courtesy : Google photos

Is duniya mein bahut si cheezein hain jo samajhayi nahin ja saktin.

(TALAASH)

Courtesy : Aamir Khan @ Twitter

13

Aamir Khan : An Exclusive Interview

"To Entertain the audience is never easy"

One of the finest and widely appreciated actors of India and one, who has proven his acting prowess in almost all of his films, Aamir Khan is always committed to his cause, thanks to the selection of the story in his films. Even in his most popular television show "Satyameva Jayate", the audience appreciated Amir immensely, because of the burning issues he raised in different episodes. His sole purpose with film making is to entertain the spectators.

However Amir admits that it is never easy to entertain the audience across the country and globe in mass. In the same breath, he further says that he never does any film just for giving any message to the society. It is well and good, if the audience gets any message as such, while getting the entertainment, which, according to him, is his first and fore-most responsibility. Aamir Khan spoke at length with me during an exclusive interview at his residence in Mumbai. Here are the excerpts of that interview-

In your views how much impact does a film create on the society?

Of course, films do make a lot impact on the society. If any topic is depicted effectively in the films, it leaves a positive impact. However, if any topic is portrayed in a wrong way that would make a rather negative impact either. So it depends upon the presentation as such. For instance, the way women are portrayed in most of our movies, it is quite objectionable. Definitely, that makes a very wrong imprint in the minds of the youth. After watching these films, the youth tend to carry an impression, as if this is the only acceptable way to treat the woman in general. But we all know, the way women are depicted in most of the Indian films, it obviously leaves a very wrong impact in the society. Of course the mature audience does not get affected with such a not-so-good depiction, that of a woman character. It apparently means that when we show good things in films, it would make a positive impact in the society. Of course story also plays a very vital role in this process.

You mentioned the importance of story. But how much?

Basically it is the story, which builds moral values in the society. When you tell good stories to a child, the characters of that story inspire the child. When a tough situation or a testing time arises in the story, how the character confronts with that situation and how did he overcome that situation? And in the end what did he get? The child then realizes that when similar situation arises in his real life, he would also overcome that situation in the same way.

So it very much clear that a good story does build character in the children. Unfortunately, in the contemporary era, we happen to give less importance to the stories.

Stories affect not merely children, but also the adults. We have seen this phenomenon, in the case of your popular movie "TAARE ZAMEEN PE". What is your opinion?

Of course, I do agree. Incidentally, "TAARE JAMEEN PE" film was not simply based on Dyslexia. Primarily, this film is based on good parenting. Even if a child is not suffering from any disease like Dyslexia, good parenting is essential. The main idea of that film was to depict, how you treat your child and how is your relationship with the child. In addition to this, the film also shows as to how you should allow your child to build his or her own personality and identity. This is very important.

I would like to mention another film of mine "RANG DE BASANTI". That movie had created a lot of positive impact in the minds of the youth especially. The impact of such an off-beat film is not seen immediately. Rather, it is seen only after a period of time

But how?

See, when children would watch this film, they might not understand the actual message of the film immediately. However, the scenes and dialogues of the film would remain alive in their minds. And after a period of time those scenes and dialogues would definitely leave their impression among them. Take the example the agitation of Anna Hajare a couple of years back. Nobody would have ever imagined that thousands of people across the country would come to street voluntarily. It is quite understandable, that these people would have inspired with any of the previous films, based on such a social issue. When the agitation began, they realized that they should also unite against the social injustice. This inner urge inspired them to join Anna's agitation. So it very much an established fact, that films do create an impression in the hearts and minds of the audience. But it is manifested in different ways, in every phase of life. If the message of a story is positive, its impact would also be in the same way.

Do you believe that if any message is given through films to the society, that would leave a better impact?

Of course. The message of story does leave an impact among the audience. More often than not, people ask me, as to whether I keep the relevant major social issues in mind while making a film. My answer is – no, I never keep any such issues in mind during my film making. My first and foremost responsibility is to entertain the audience. When the spectators come to the theatre hall, they do not expect that we would give them any message. For getting message they would better go to schools and colleges. They come to theatre simply to get the entertainment. And we must respect this very choice of our spectators. Let me tell you, it is never an easy job to entertain the spectators as a whole.

As far as my job is concerned, I select a story on the basis of my interest and preference. I normally choose a story, which entertains me from within and which inspires me to get connected with the characters or incidents. It may happen that such story would not have any message either. But my getting connected with that story is very important for my selection. If that story has any message it is well and good. In fact it is a bonus.

But I never choose any story after lot of thinking and planning as such. The kind of person I am, it is very much certain, that I never compromise with my choice of stories. When I had heard the story of TAARE ZAMEEN PE", I liked with very much. When the film was ready for release, many people came to me and said, what is the sense of making a film on Dyslexia? Will you get any audience for this film? This was the impression. Similarly for LAGAAN also nobody was ready to join me in making this film. Since my natural inclination has always been towards such off-beat things, I liked that story and fascinated me as well.

So how do you choose any story for your film?

See, when I choose any story I never keep the choice of the audience in my mind. Because how can I decide, as to what they would like or dislike. If is obviously for them to decide. So, at best, I can think of my own choice and preference. For me, a film means to devote two precious years of my life wholeheartedly. And after completing that film and spending two years of my life, I ask with myself as to what kind of inner enrichment I got out of this film? And what future vision or thought I carry forward from this film?

I challenge myself as to whether I have learnt anything from my film or not? And whether or not,

I got entertained from that film? If the film proves to be successful, my satisfaction and rejoice get doubled. But I never compromise in story selection because of these things.

Do you feel that only a good story would not be sufficient for the success of any film. Its effective presentation on the screen is equally important?

See, any creative individual can perform the best, only when he or she enjoys the work. Unless you are excited and thrilled while doing your work, the outcome would not be that fantastic and extra ordinary. I would like give you an example of my latest film- DANGAL. It is based on the story of a wrestler's family in Haryana. The film also has a social impact. The family of famous wrestler Mahavir Singh Phogat has four daughters. Two of them have won Gold medals in Commonwealth Games.

The film highlights, the struggle of this middle-class family, where the father groomed his two daughters in odd conditions and limited resources. Yet they both emerged as champions and brought laurels to the country. I feel this success story can inspire anyone and everyone. I am quite confident and convinced that this story is truly an original one and its presentation on the screen would have to be equally creative. Dangal got tremendous response.

□

Epilogue

There is no two ways about the magnitude of impact that the cinema has on Indian people. Sheer common sense dictates that a medium as wide-reaching as cinema is bound to create some flux and leave some imprint on the minds of its viewers. It is an attempts to illustrate the positive change that a movie icon can play in framing the mindset of a society. However, there is an important caveat here. Since filmstars wield such an important power and may control over the society, they also have to bear the burden of an associated responsibility as well.

Filmmakers, through their impactful and meaningful cinema, helped in giving a widespread direction to the progression of the society. It is said that cinema is a mirror of the society. The causal link between cinema and society is such that society is the cause and the cinematic content is the effect. However, in case of these filmmakers, the reverse was also true. More than often, these filmmakers shaped the society by way of their films. There are several institutions in India which propagate filmmaking and the technicalities behind it. These institutions provide a thrust to the vocation of cinema as a viable employment, often adding a course correction in the journey-destination of cinema. In this way, it was seen that how cinema impacts the socio-economic profile of a country and its societal components.

A profiling of Aamir Khan's filmography showed the transition that Aamir Khan has made as a movie star and the kind of films he has been associated with. It is important to understand that the certain filmstars have emerged as an icons. These icons play an important role in shaping the society and the perceptions occurring en masse. The social impact can only be imputed, but such a great contribution can and should not be ignored.

Taking up 3 films as an, the attempt was to understand how a films as a medium can communicate different social issues. The issues might range from national integrity, injustice to emotional connect, parental linkages; however, the entire coverage can be dealt with in a socially responsible manner that can influence the society and its denizens positively.

His films and show not just create awareness about the various issues, but to also chart a way forward, a compromise, a resolution.

Regarding satyemev jayate Aamir himself once

said," I might not be able to solve all your problems but I can hold your hand hug you and make you feel better.' After all, it was the thought that counted in the end. With the show, the crusa-der's focus was not just on the classes or a certain part of society but on the whole nation. He could have chosen the simpler path of making a movie rather than taking up the challenge of making Indians dedicate their Sunday morning to an engaging, insightful yet grueling talk show. But then he is a public figure with a difference!

If he continues being a part of such responsible cinema, Aamir Khan would well be on his way in proving the adage "one man can't make a difference" wrong.

□

I Sum It Up

Aamir is a Perfectionist to the core. He is also known to be aware of the pulse of the audience. He also is the most uncompromising producer-director. The Midas Touch that he wields when acting or producing directing films is the reason why his last few films find a place in the all time chartbusters. His high success rate is a heady mix of research, analysis and visualization.

Filmlore says that when Rajkumar Hirani approached him for 3 idiots for the role of Rancho who is 20 years younger than his age, Aamir took his time to decide whether he could essay the role and finally decided to respect the director's verdict of casting him for the role and the rest is history. But he had done everything possible to visualize whether he could essay the college going role. He would also play badminton during the shoot to make him look like the student he was made out to be. Such is his conviction and it usually pays off.

Aamir feels like his audience not like a celebrity. Even during his script sessions he is known to laugh, cry, questions and applauds like the audience in a cinema. He then consents if he feels that the audience would love his role. In this he would not look at the size of the role but only the impact.

So, when people complain that Aamir does too few films, and that when he does them, he 'interferes' and takes a lot of time and effort, they must appreciate the fact that it is his single-minded focus that has stood him in good stead over the years. And we hope that is something Aamir Khan will not let go of for the years to come. He does not want to lose creative control over the project hence does only one project at a time and then takes it to the end as he visualized it. He also takes out time before he essays the role to research, identify traits and characteristics of the role and also sees actors who have done similar roles. In the case of Satyamev Jayate too, he toured different parts of the country and interacted with people to identify issues to portray.

He doesn't mind putting his eggs in the baskets of new directors. If the content is good, he would go for it. He would also not use his star value to promote the film if he is not in it. In the case of Delhi Belly, Peepli Live and Dhobi Ghat, he did not promote the movie because he did not want to and also he laid his faith on new directors.

He also is a marketing genius. This fact is proven because he uses techniques that have not been used in the market before. He used disguises for the promotion of 3 idiots and would go out in public in Varanasi without being spotted. The media came to know of it only after he left. His radio cutout of PK too raised eyebrows but became a rage. His black hat during public appearances during Dhoom 3 and tattoos to promote Ghajini are trend setters too. He was found cutting hair on the wayside and doing such odd jobs to promote his films.

All in all he creates news to promote his movies. Such is the enigma... Aamir.

References

Gajjar, M. (2007). *BBC – Shropshire – Bollywood – Taare Zameen Par. Bbc.co.uk*. Retrieved 27 September 2014, from http://www.bbc.co.uk/shropshire/films/bollywood/2007/12/taare_zameen_review.shtml

Indiatoday.intoday.in (2013), *Aamir Khan clarifies Taare Zameen Par row at Agenda Aaj Tak: Agenda Aaj Tak 2013, News – India Today*, Retrieved 16 September 2014, from http://indiatoday.intoday.in/story/aamir-khan-clarifies-taare-zameen-par-row-with-amol-gupte/1/327858.html

Jha, S. (2007). *BNS News Items. Bollywoodnewsservice.com*. Retrieved 27 September 2014, from http://www.bollywoodnewsservice.com/subhash_k_jha/archive.php?article_id=478

Jha, S. (2009). *Life's worth living with 3 Idiots – The Times of India. The Times of India*. Retrieved 27 September 2014, from http://timesofindia.indiatimes.com/entertainment/hindi/bollywood/news-interviews/lifes-worth-living-with-3-idiots/articleshow/5377572.cms

John Nugent, *The DVD Discount Bin: Lagaan Redux,Trenton Independent*, 1 April 2011, p. B2.

Kamath, S. (2007). *Scoring sixers with every scene.*

Thehindu.com. Retrieved 27 September 2014, from http://www.thehindu.com/2001/06/29/stories/0929022j.htm

Kazmi, N. (2009). *3 Idiots – The Times of India. The Times of India*. Retrieved 27 September 2014, from http://timesofindia.indiatimes.com/entertainment/hindi/movie-review/3-Idiots/movie-review/5373913.cms

Masand, R. (2007). *Review: Taare Zameen Par may change your life. IBN Live*. Retrieved 27 September 2014, from http://ibnlive.in.com/news/review-taare-zameen-par-may-change-your-life/54724-17.html

U2140161.nettech.net.in,.(2009). *MOVIE DESCRIPTION*. Retrieved 27 September 2014, from http://u2140161.nettech.net.in/pramod-assignment/pramod-assignment-I/pramod-favorite/movie%20plot.html